*May the Lord
knock your
socks off every
time you read and
hear His word.*

# HOW ANYONE CAN MAKE

# MONEY

# FROM THE STOCK MARKETS

ROLAND LACHANCE

# HOW ANYONE CAN MAKE MONEY FROM THE STOCK MARKETS

*Written by*

# Roland Lachance

*Author and owner of*

## Walk The Talk Ministries

authorHOUSE®

AuthorHouse™
1663 Liberty Drive
Bloomington, IN 47403
www.authorhouse.com
Phone: 1 (800) 839-8640

Published by AuthorHouse   09/21/2018

ISBN: 978-1-4918-1838-1 (sc)
ISBN: 978-1-4918-1837-4 (hc)
ISBN: 978-1-4918-1836-7 (e)

Library of Congress Control Number: 2013917270

# CONTENTS

# ACKNOWLEDGMENTS

First and foremost I wish to give all the glory, honor, and praises to the Father, Son, and Holy Ghost for this entire book; from the cover to every place and person the Lord sent across my path. Truly without them none of this would have been possible.

I would like to acknowledge my wife, my daughter and my son for always being there for me during my rough years of learning all these things the hard way.

# CONTRIBUTORS

To everyone the Lord used from the least who persecuted me daily, even to the greatest Angelic massagers the Lord used to minister to me.

The Ryrie Study Bible; By Charles Ryrie. Copyright ©1978, Moody Bible Institute of Chicago Moody Press. Used with permission. This was the bible that I used throughout this book. Out of all the bibles I have read, this one was more alive to me. God's Word jumped out of its pages onto me after prayer. Special thanks to Jennie Sawyer for Janet McVay Editorial Assistant, to whom gave me permission to copy God's Word.

Special thanks to Pastor Cheal who helped me with some editing and kept me planted, watered and humble.

I am most thankful and grateful for My Lord and Savior in using me in putting this book together and in helping me not to limit Him in what you have before you today. Amen . . .

# Warning!

It has been noted that anyone who reads and hears everything written in this book, may result in changes in their understanding, finances, health and anyone around them.

# SECTION ONE:

# WHAT, WHEN, WHERE AND WHY THIS BOOK

# INTRODUCTION

Greetings to those who are called of God and to His church: grace be to you and peace from God our Father, and from the Lord Jesus Christ. In Pro. 5: 23 it says, "**He shall die without instruction: and in the greatness of his folly he shall go astray.**" God's word is talking about you and me here: without the right instruction we shall die. When it comes to money, most people I know say one thing and do something else; and if they know anything their not saying.

My first 900 page hard cover book is called God's Instructions from Walk the Talk Ministries. It holds 100 lessons on how to hear God's voice or to getting answers to all of your prayers. You might say, My thirst and hunger for His instructions grew more and more and He revealed unto me, the mysteries of His word in ways I've never seen or heard taught anywhere. Although anyone can download this book for $3.99 onto their tablet or E- Reader. In my heart I would rather give it away for free to anyone the Lord sends across my path.

Most of the books I have read about making money came from writers who never invested their own money and could never grantee that you would make any. Some of the books I read told me that those who had money, it was like pulling teeth to get any of it, because there was nothing in it for them.

Some of the books I read talked about malty millionaires who had more money than they know what to do with; and had some kind of void or something missing in their lives and it wasn't until they found God and His word that made the void go away.

So then I began thinking, what if someone has the Lord in their life, but their void is money. If worse comes to worse and I give them what the Lord gave me to make money. Then when they have all the money they could ever need to get their lives complete, then they could always get my other books to round off any other voids they might have. There is nothing wrong with loving God and having money to pay your bills off and to help other people with.

It's when you put the love of money before God; that makes all the difference. In Mt. 6: 24 Jesus said, **"No man can serve two masters: for either he will hate the one, and love the other; or else he will hold to the one, and despise the other. ye cannot serve God and mammon."** God did not answer all of my questions, but He answered the ones I needed to go forward. Just like this book will not answer all of your questions, but if you use what God gives you, He will give you more. If you have a real hunger or thirst for Gods instructions and are serious about it, then this book is a must for you. My desire now, is to get these same instructions to you that He gave to me and see how God blesses you. Amen. . .

God bless you two folds

*Brother Roland*

# How To Use This Book

Good morning. Grace be to you and peace from God our Father and from the Lord Jesus Christ. In Act. 10: 34 it says, **"God is no respecter of persons:"** It doesn't matter if you are male or female, big or little, black or white, foreign or domestic, what's important is your thirst and hunger for God's instructions, and you have taken the first step. Jesus said it best when He told His disciples, **"The word ye hear is not mine, but the Father's which sent me."** (Jn. 14: 24)

God woke me up in the middle of the night so you can get this message hot off the press. I know without any doubt whatsoever God has done for me and still is, He can do for you. In Pro. 8: 33-34 it says, You need to hear God's instructions to be wise and blessed. This means when you are reading this book you also need to hear it. If you put God first, He will put you first. When you read this letter and all of God's instructions out loud, try to be all alone by yourself, because the devil will use anything and anybody to steal God's instructions away from you.

There is something you must do before you are blessed like I was with these instructions and that is, you must ask the Lord to open your eyes, ears, and understanding onto this book and all of His instructions before you go any further with this letter and God's instructions.

In Jas. 4: 2 it says, **"Ye have not, because ye ask not."** If you don't ask, He does not have to do it. I certainly can't do it for you.

The bottom line is how serious are you? This prayer must come from your heart: and if you want to be wise and blessed, then do so right now.

Whenever the Lord uses me to do a Bible study or to preach from His pulpit, He has me prepare His people to receive His instructions. He's telling me right now to prepare you in the same manner. If you're reading this letter just to hear me, you're wasting your time and God's. But if you are reading and hearing God's instructions to see and hear what God wants to tell and show you, then God will knock your socks off!

This book has only one lesson. Lesson # 110. If you want to know more about God and His word, you need to get one of the other books that He gave me to write. This book or lesson is to teach you how to make your money make more money. I can only say this, That I am a true source or someone who uses these instructions every day and have not lost any of my own money as long as I followed all of God's instructions to the letter. I have made most of the mistakes so you don't have to. As you hear and see His instructions and start using and applying them each and every day in your walk with God your life will never be the same. Amen. . .

I love you in the lord always.

*Brother Roland*

# Section Two:

## How Anyone Can Make Money From The Stock Markets

From
Roland Lachance

# CHAPTER ONE

# You need money to make money

In Proverbs 13: 22 God's word says, **"A good man leaveth an inheritance to his children's children: and the wealth of the sinner is laid up for the just."** If you are someone who does not do everything this book instructs you to do, then the wealth of the sinners may not be laid up for you. I am talking about your own personal money tree, or a place you can go to anytime you need money.

If you are someone who does not need money and dislikes following instructions, then just stop reading this book and give it to someone who will. You can always go back to doing whatsoever you were doing before you got this book. A just person will not only follow the instructions given in this book to the letter, but will not let pride or greed get in the way of letting their money make money for them.

The money that you need to help you make money is not going to fall out of the sky right into your lap. Unless you were born with a silver spoon in your mouth or married to someone who has lots of money or part of the privileged elite, you have to work for it.

In order to make the money you want there are things that need to be done and they are not going to get done all by their self. Until you treat this like a real job or an investment for your future retirement no one can do it for you. Ask yourself, What would I do so I can quit my job and live anywhere I want, do anything I want and go anywhere I want whenever I want in less than five years? When you are ready to go forward, just turn to the next page.

The first thing you need to do is find a place for your money to make more money for you. Just pick up a phone book and look for a brokerage firm in your area or go on line. If you don't have internet service or a computer you can go to your local library and use one of theirs. With today's technology you can do almost everything on a smart phone. You are not looking for an investment adviser; only a safe place to buy and sell stocks. By the way, this new job or business will allow you to deduct your computer, phone, printer, paper, internet service and any other expenses including this book you are reading and hearing can be written off on your taxes. You need to be looking at the bigger picture.

Some brokerage firms will let you open an account with as little as $500.00 dollars; but, the more money you have the cheaper your commission will be. I've seen them go from nothing to more than $11.00 dollars per trade. A trade is anytime you buy or sell a stock you pay that dollar amount or commission every time you make a trade, weather you buy or sell one stock or a thousand stocks. That's how any brokerage firm makes money whenever we use their trading tools and every time a stock is bought or sold.

A good broker who works for a brokerage firm; will take your money and buy and sell as many stocks that he or she can; so that at the end of the year, they will show that they made 5 or 10% more money for you. While keeping all of the commissions they made for their company and their own personal gain. A bad broker, will do the same thing, but will show a lost at the end of the year; because they did not know what they were doing.

When you find a place that will work with you, the first thing you have to do is open an (Rollover) or I R A Brokerage Account. Otherwise, every time you sell a stock, you have to pay a large tax on any monies your money made for you. This means that you will have less money in your account to make more money for you. The only time you have to pay taxes on your I R A retirement account is when you take your money out of your account.

Your money is safe in this account until you reach the age of seventy years old then you will be forced to take a portion out every year for retirement; or the government will take it out for you. If you have a 401k or any other type of retirement account that you can roll over into this new I R A Brokerage account do so at this time. If you let the brokerage firm do everything for you; remember this one thing, The only way they make money is from the commissions they get when a stock is bought or sold. Any retirement account that you have that the brokerage firm is making money off of your expense needs to stop. From now on you want to be the one doing the buying, selling and managing all of your transactions yourself. (No one needs to know your business.)

This will be tax free money that you will be trading with and the only time you pay taxes on that money is when you take it out of your account. If you don't have a retirement account and you are 50 years old or less, you can open one with no more than $5,000.00 dollars per year. If you are over the age of 50, the most you can open one with is 6, 000.00 dollars per year.

This money is tax differed from your annual income for that year only. Then every year you can tax defer another five or six thousand. It's almost like having free none taxable money to make money with. The more money you have to trade with the sooner you can retire. If you are married, then you can open up two accounts and have twice the tax free money to trade with.

Until you start trading, place your money in a Money Market Fund. Your money will make money for you even if you just leave it in there and don't use it; they will give you interest on your money every year as long as you keep it in the money market account. The same way your bank would do for you if you kept your money in their bank.

When you are ready to make a trade move the money from the Money Market Fund to whatever stock you want to purchase. Any time your money is not making money for you, it should go back into the Money Market Fund.

When you want to know how much money you have available to trade with, just check your Money Market Fund account. Whenever you sell your stock(s), instruct your broker to place your money back into your Money Market Fund. This process may take three to five business days before it becomes free and clear every time you sell a stock. If you attempt to buy and sell a stock before you have sufficient funds available, they can and will shut you down up to ninety days or longer. This is why it's so important to wait three to five days for your funds to be free and clear so you have more money to buy and trade with.

You can trade by phone with your broker or do it yourself on line, which I have found to be a faster way to get your trade completed. There may be times when you may want to sell or buy a stock or stocks from another exchange from another country or from a clip board that has a new stock to trade; this may be a good time to have your broker do it for you. To make that kind of trade they require an extra commission to the other exchange; or they may charge you $50.00 dollars for every 500 shares you buy or sell. Every exchange has their own way of doing things spicily if you live in a different country.

By the way, if you buy a specialty stock from a clip board or some other exchange it may take 5 minutes or longer for that trade to take place but, when you want to sell that stock, it may take forever to sell; do to the small amount of volume. Needless to say, I learned this lesson the hard way. Before you can buy or sell any stock and make money from your trade; you must learn to first walk before you can run.

# CHAPTER TWO

# Finding the right stocks to buy and sell

T he first criteria in finding the right stock to buy and sell would be to find a stock that has been around for ten years or longer. Like the brand name of your favorite food, shoe store, restaurant or company that's been around for a long time and not planning to go away at any time soon.

In order to avoid any copy rights or brand names, I will use BR or Brother Roland (BR) for all of the charts in this book. This way you will be looking at charts drown up by me to illustrate or show you what I'm talking about. On the next page you will find two examples of what to look for. On page 16, chart # 1 shows you where BR has been around for less than 3 years. I've been told that more than 50% of new company's die or go bankrupt within the first two years.

You want to find stocks that's been around for a while, not here today and gone tomorrow. Like # 2 and # 3 charts on page 17. Because of 911 many stocks took a mud dive as you can see to the right of the graph where the number four is on page 21. Please take a minute and study this page and get familiar with where everything is you need to know about what your stock did fifteen minutes ago, all the way to when it first started. This 35 year chart for Brother Roland (BR) is only an imaginary stock used to illustrate the kind of chart you're looking for, and is not one of over 8,000 stocks you can pull up on the computer.

# #1 CHART

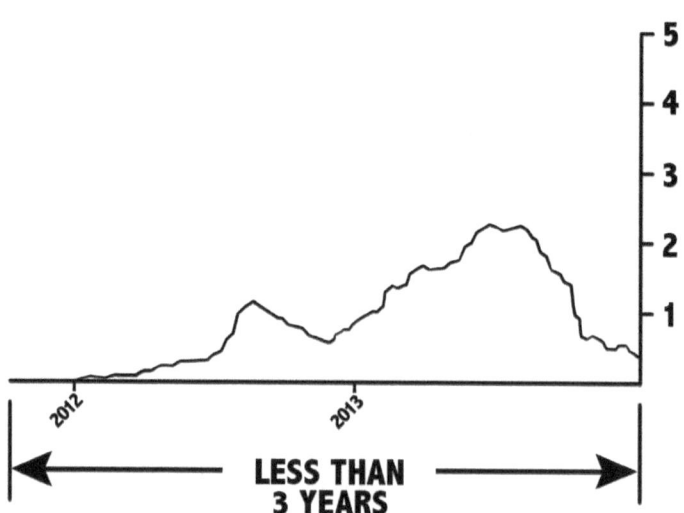

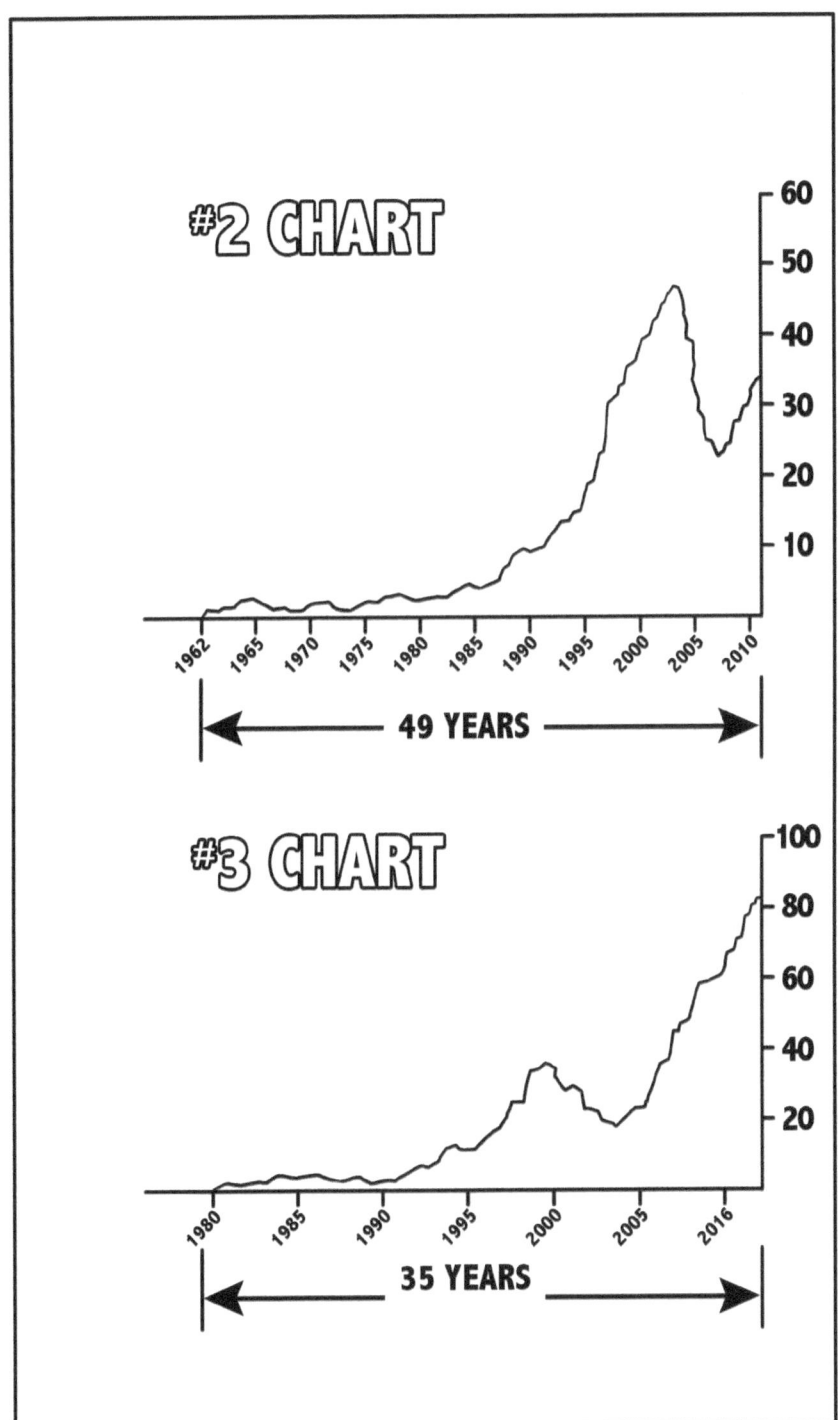

When I first started out, all I had to do was go to any web browser or search engine and click on Daily finance and it took me to a financial page. I went to the local library and found out that the internet has changed a lot since then. If you go to the top of your web browser or search engine page, type http: www. (Place your web browser or Search engine name here.) .com / quotes / (Then put a stock name or symbol here.) / ? And hit enter; you might get a page that looks like page 19 that has a graph on it.

If it does not take you to a financial or summary page there is a good chance you may have to use the tools from the web pages of your brokerage firm. Ask your broker, how to get a page like the one you see on page 19. From that page you will find a place that looks like the top left hand where you can get a quote or search for any stock, with a box next to it. Just put in a company's name or symbol in the box and then click (Get Quotes) or (Go).

When you get a picture of a graph and right below that graph you can click on a day or year, just pick one. It will look something like the graph that is on page 19. You may have to ask your broker, how or where you need to go on your computer to find a graph like the one you see on the next page. If you click anywhere on the graph it should tell you what that stock did on that day.

Every brokerage firm has their own set of charts and graphs; they may look different or found in a different location on their web page, but everything you need to make money should all be the same. Ask your broker, where you need to go to buy, sell and to execute any trades. Every brokerage firm has their own web page to do this on.

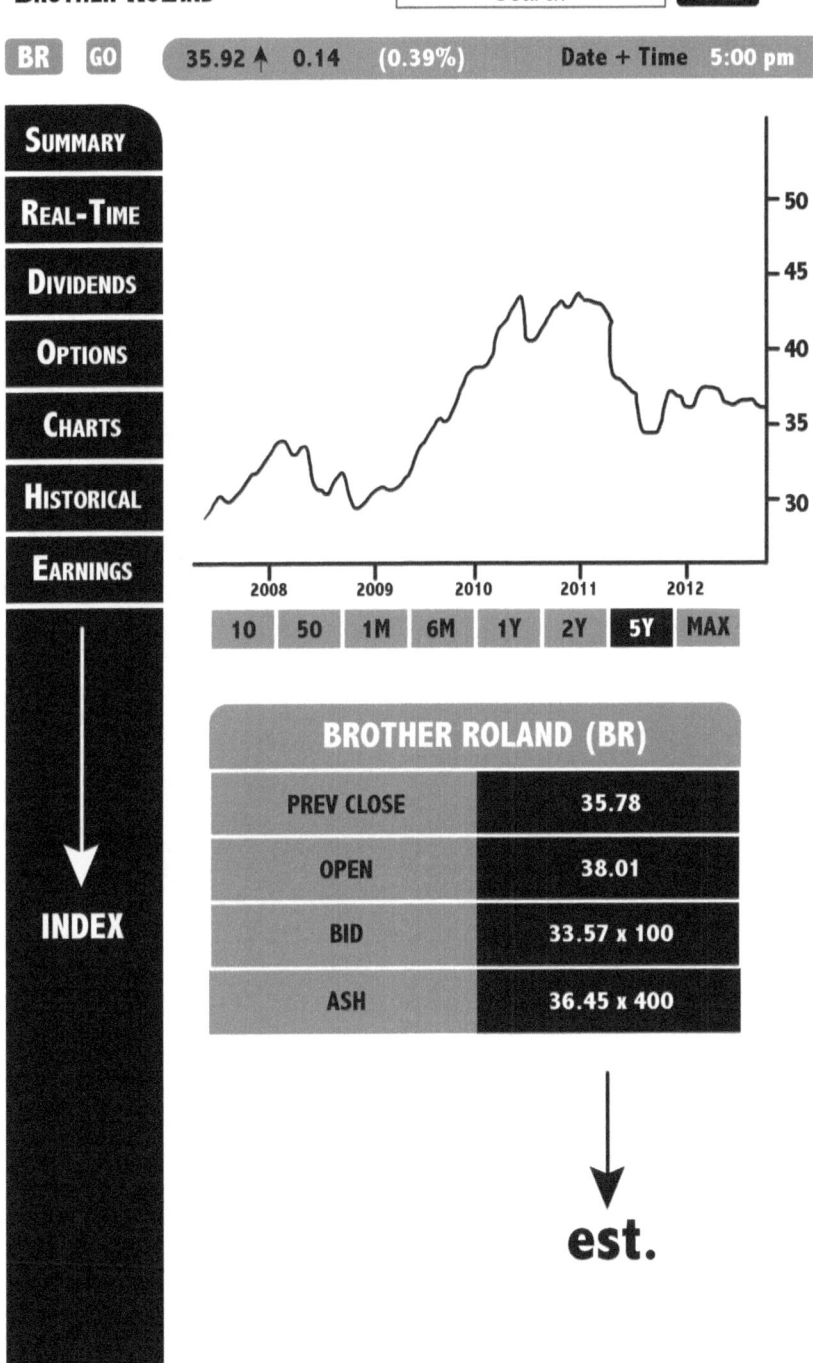

BROTHER ROLAND

Search    WEB

BR  GO    35.92 ↑  0.14   (0.39%)        Date + Time   5:00 pm

SUMMARY

REAL-TIME

DIVIDENDS

OPTIONS

CHARTS

HISTORICAL

EARNINGS

2008      2009      2010      2011      2012

| 10 | 50 | 1M | 6M | 1Y | 2Y | 5Y | MAX |

INDEX

| BROTHER ROLAND (BR) | |
|---|---|
| PREV CLOSE | 35.78 |
| OPEN | 38.01 |
| BID | 33.57 x 100 |
| ASH | 36.45 x 400 |

est.

1) This is where you will find the name of the stock you are looking at. Following the name is the symbol or letter(s) used to identify the stock you're looking at.

2) This indicates a dollar amount your stock can go to.

3) This indicates where the stock was at the date indicated.

4) This shows what the stock did from the start 35 years ago up to 15 minutes ago.

5) You can click anywhere on this bar to find a picture of a graph that shows you what the stock did one month ago, all the way down to the beginning when the stock was first started.

6) This tells you where the stock is trading at right now. To the right of this dollar amount you can see what your stock made or lost since the market opened.

7) This tells you where the stock closed the day before, where it opened at the start of the trading day, it even tells you the 52 week low and high your stock did. All of these figures are constantly being updated throughout the day.

8) This is your page index. You can click on anything from quotes to a balance sheet. Anything you want to know about your stock can be found here.

9) This is where you can check different stocks using the same chart. Just put in the new stock cymbal or name and click (Get Chart.) or (Go) button.

10) This is when you want to get a quotes on any other stock. Just put in the new stock cymbal or name and then click on (Get Quotes.) Right below this is a indicator showing you how the Dow and Nasdaq are doing.

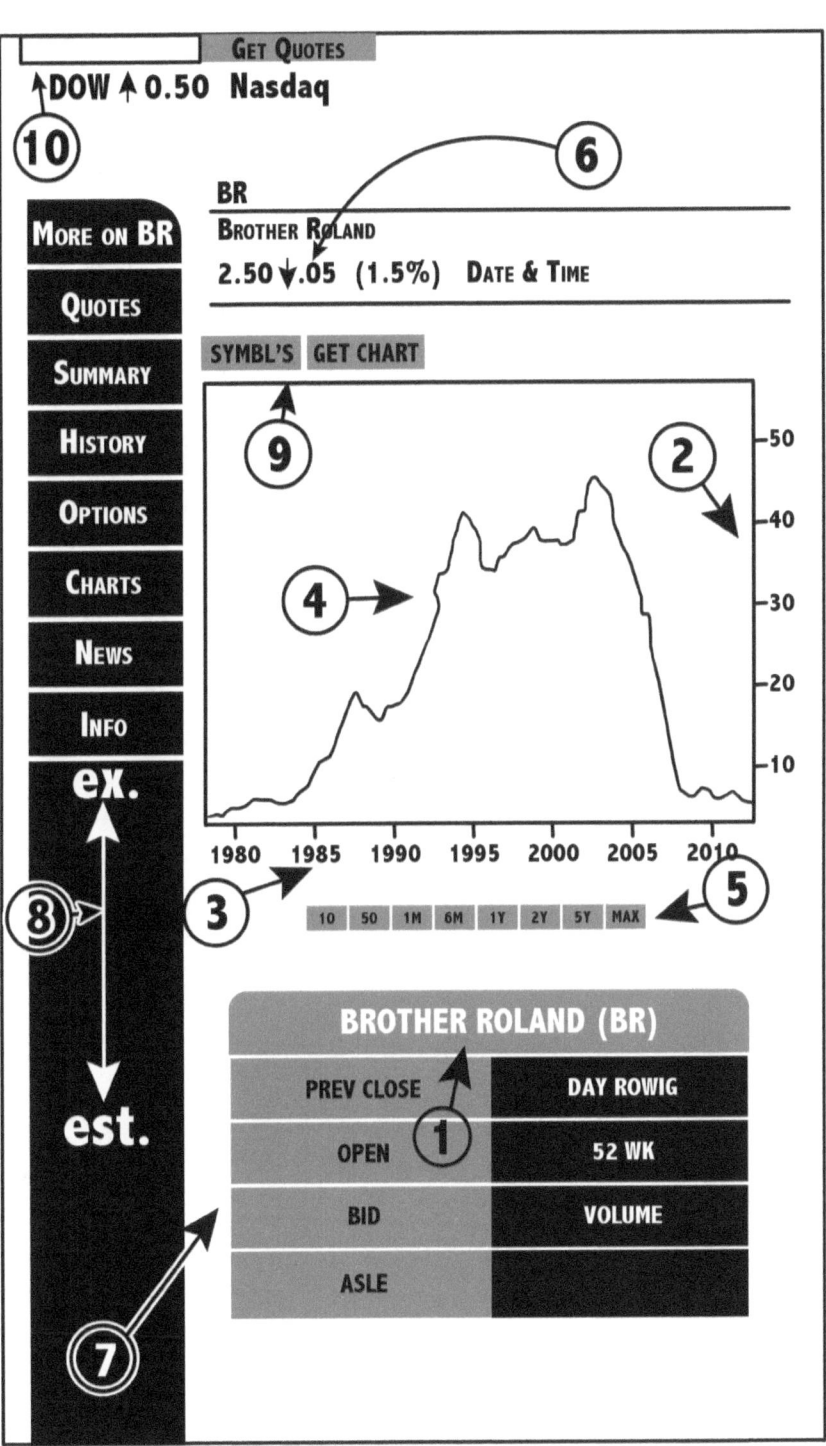

I have taken the time to mark off the important places for you to familiarize yourself with. Every Brokerage firm has its own finance or summary page. When you find the right charts or graphs that work for you, then click on that page and send it to your favorites file on your computer and when you want to use it just click on favorites.

You will be looking for a chart or graph that you can work with. I have found out that every sight is deferent. Where the graph may be on the bottom of the page instead of the upper right hand corner and Get quotes, may be found anywhere on the page.

## CHAPTER THREE

# You want to find stocks that have a dividend

Y our next criteria is to find stocks that have a dividend or set amount that will be paid to the shareholders of that stock. Some stocks payout once a year and others quarterly. The set amount can be .01 to $4.00 dollars or more each time for every stock you own. If you're going to buy and sell stocks, you might as well buy stocks that have dividends. This allows you to have more money to make money with.

You can buy or sell any stocks that does not have a dividend payout; but I have found out that many stocks that have dividends, when that company is not doing very well they will change the payout amount to almost nothing or even stop all together.

Part of my portfolio consists of having over 50 stocks that pays out a dividend. I only buy three stocks if it is priced under $50.00 dollars and one if the stock is more than $50.00 dollars. (No more than 10% of your whole portfolio should go into this.)

Never keep all your eggs in one basket. This is also a good place to keep a small amount of your money for three reasons.

1) The dividends will give you 5% or more on the money you keep in the stocks you are holding.

2) If the stock you're in take's a mud dive or because you did not have enough funds available when you made your trade. This is where you can find the money you need to make it right.

3) Anytime I look at my portfolio I can see what all of my stocks are doing at the same time. If any of your stocks stop paying dividends, you can sell that stock and get a new one for your trades.

One of the first couples I gave these instructions too, after five years they were making enough money to retire on from the dividends payouts they were making every year. If they have followed all of the same instructions that are in this book, this money is only 10% of their portfolio which is only one way to make money to retire on.

Go to your brokerage accounts summary page, or click on your favorites page that look like page (25.)

Let's have a look, shall we?

This quote page is quoting Brother Roland (BR). As you can see on the top left hand corner of the page. Right below the Company name is a box where you can put any stock you want and click on go. Then all you have to do is click on dividends: located on the index column of page 25 and something like the example you have on page 27 will come up.

If you can't find it on that page, type in dividends. It should look something like page 27. If you still can't find it ask your Brokerage firm how to find it on their web site. You will save lots of time by placing this page site on your favorites list or even better by placing it on a short cut by making an (app.) on the screen when you turn your computer on. So all you have to do is click on that app. and this will save you lots of time when you are looking for the right stock to put into your portfolio. Click on dividends and you will get a page that looks like page (27.)

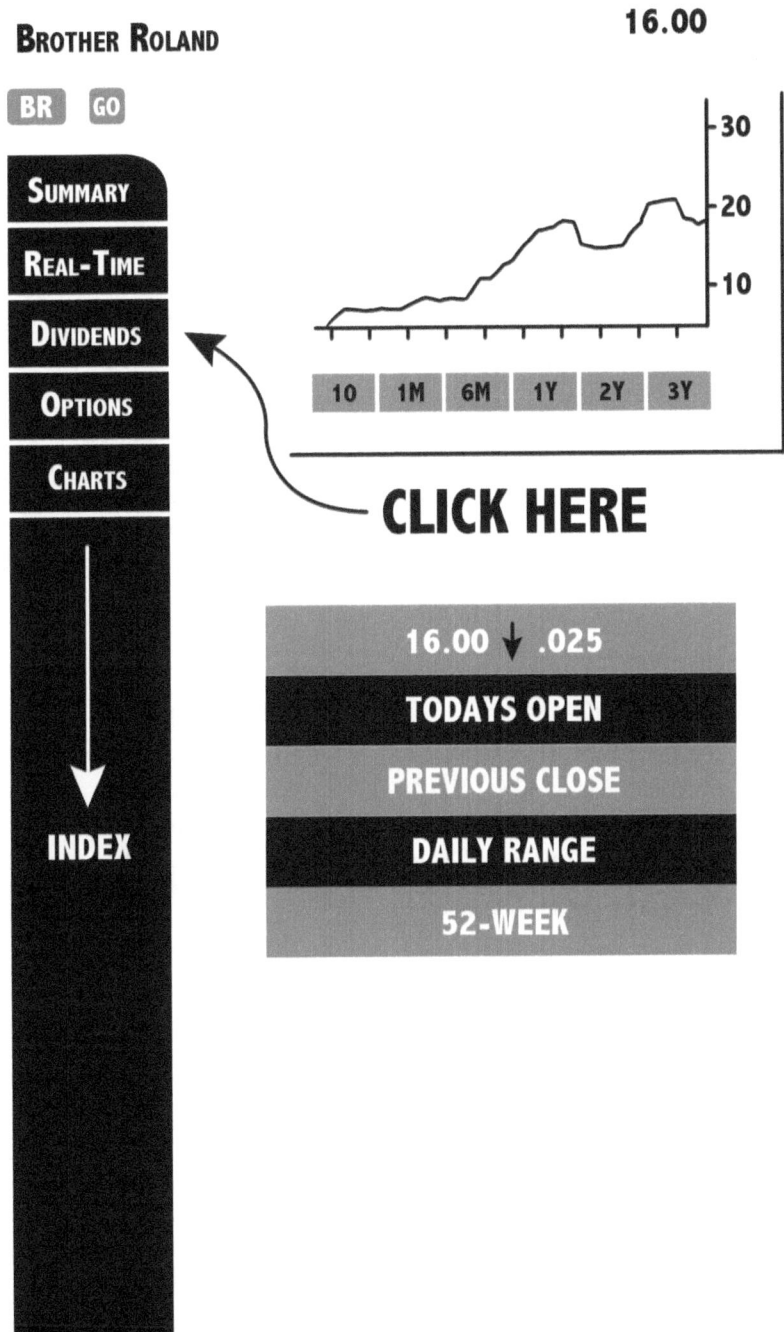

Every stock is different; as well as the time you need to own them.

1) This is where you find the name of the stock you're looking at.

2) This is where you would go to change the stock you want to look at. All you would do is type in the new name or symbol of the stock you want and then click go.

3) This is your index to where you can go back to the summary page you was just on or anywhere else you want to go to.

4) This is the date that you make money if you don't sell that stock until the following day after that date.

5) This tells you how much money the stock will make on each share or stocks you own.

6) This is the date you must already own the stock. You must buy this stock one day before that date in order to make money on this dividend.

Let's say you bought 1,000 shares of (BR) Brother Roland Company stock on 6/12/ 2011 and you sold it on 7/11/2011, how much money did your money make for you?

$$1,000 \times .32 = 320.00$$

What would you have made if the dividend was .50 or 1.00?

$$1,000 \times .50 = 500.00$$
$$1,000 \times 1.00 = 1,000.00$$

Your 29 day investment made you 320.00 dollars. This might be more than what your bank is giving you for your money, but it's not enough for you to retire on. . .

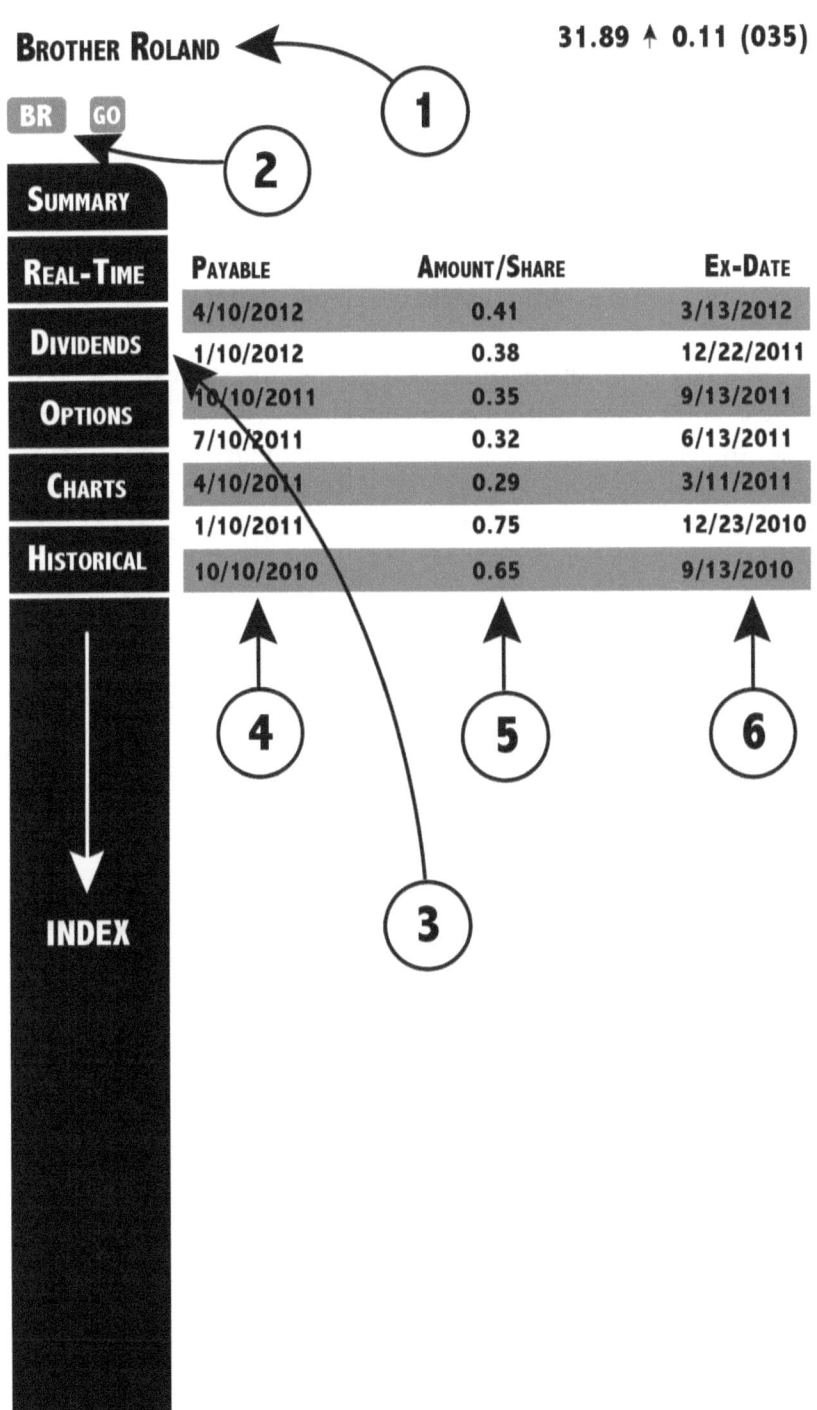

When you find a page like this one, you might want to place that page onto your favorites list. This page sight will also have a place where you can get quotes on any other stock as well. Any of the charts I show you can be printed on your printer by simply right clicking on your mouse and click on print. If you right click on the graph, your printer should only print out the graph for you.

Let's look at another example shall we?

So if you buy 1,000 shares of Brother Roland, Inc. Stock on 3/11/2012 and sold 1,000 shares of Brother Roland Stocks on 4/11/2012 how much money did your money make with a .41 cent dividend?

$$1,000 \times .41 = 410.00 \text{ dollars}$$

How much money would you have made if you sold 500 shares of Brother Roland, Stock on 4/09/ 2012 and 500 shares of Brother Roland, Inc. Stock on 4/13/2012 how much money did your money make with a .41 cent dividend?

$$500 \times .41 = 205.00 \text{ dollars}$$

In order to make money from any dividends, you must own that stock between the dates given. As you can see the amounts change as well as dates. This stock ranges from .29 to .75 cents. I have noticed that almost every time a company pays out a dividend, the price of that stock goes down. If the stock price is lower than when you bought that stock you might want to hold onto it until it makes money for you.

Whenever a company pays out any cash amount, they will give it to you by adding more stocks to your purchase.

**BR** **GO**

| SUMMARY |
|---------|
| REAL-TIME |
| DIVIDENDS |
| OPTIONS |
| CHARTS |
| HISTORICAL |

**DIVIDEND HISTORY**

| PAYABLE | AMOUNT/SHARE | EX-DATE |
|---------|--------------|---------|
| 4/10/2012 | 0.41 | 3/13/2012 |
| 1/10/2012 | 0.38 | 12/22/2011 |
| 10/10/2011 | 0.35 | 9/13/2011 |
| 7/10/2011 | 0.32 | 6/13/2011 |
| 4/10/2011 | 0.29 | 3/11/2011 |
| 1/10/2011 | 0.75 | 12/23/2010 |
| 10/10/2010 | 0.65 | 9/13/2010 |

**est.**

**Buy one day before this date.**

**INDEX**

**Sell one day after this date.**

Let's take this one step further, shall we?

If you click on Historical Prices on the index column on the left hand side of the page, something like your next page will pop up.

**BROTHER ROLAND**

31.89 ↑ 0.11 (035)

SOLD

BR  GO

| | DATE | OPEN | HIGH | LOW | CLOSE |
|---|---|---|---|---|---|
| SUMMARY | | | | | |
| REAL-TIME | 4/12/12 | 31.21 | 31.89 | 31.10 | 31.50 |
| | 4/11/12 | 31.25 | 31.50 | 31.13 | 31.21 |
| DIVIDENDS | 4/10/12 | 31.24 | 31.49 | 31.12 | 31.20 |
| OPTIONS | 4/9/12 | 31.23 | 31.48 | 31.11 | 31.19 |
| | 4/5/12 | 31.22 | 31.47 | 31.10 | 31.18 |
| CHARTS | 4/3/12 | 31.21 | 31.46 | 31.09 | 31.17 |
| HISTORICAL | 4/2/12 | 31.20 | 31.45 | 31.08 | 31.16 |
| | 3/30/12 | 30.95 | 31.40 | 30.72 | 30.75 |
| EARNINGS | 3/29/12 | 30.94 | 31.39 | 30.71 | 30.74 |
| | 3/28/12 | 30.93 | 31.38 | 30.70 | 30.73 |
| | 3/27/12 | 30.92 | 31.37 | 30.69 | 30.72 |
| | 3/26/12 | 30.91 | 31.36 | 30.68 | 30.71 |
| | 3/23/12 | 30.90 | 31.35 | 30.67 | 30.70 |
| | 3/22/12 | 30.80 | 31.25 | 30.57 | 30.60 |
| | 3/21/12 | 30.75 | 31.20 | 30.52 | 30.55 |
| INDEX | 3/20/12 | 30.60 | 31.05 | 30.47 | 30.50 |
| | 3/19/12 | 30.59 | 31.04 | 30.48 | 30.49 |
| | 3/16/12 | 30.58 | 31.03 | 30.47 | 30.48 |
| | 3/15/12 | 30.57 | 31.02 | 30.46 | 30.47 |
| | 3/14/12 | 30.56 | 3... | 30.45 | 30.46 |
| | 3/13/12 | 30.55 | 31.00 | 30.44 | 30.45 |
| | 3/12/12 | 30.54 | 30.71 | 30.39 | 30.44 |
| | 3/9/12 | 30.53 | 30.70 | 30.40 | 30.43 |
| | 3/8/12 | 30.52 | 30.69 | 30.39 | 30.42 |

BUY

Say you buy 1,000 shares of Brother Roland Stock on 3/9/12 for $30.40 dollars a share and sold 1,000 shares of Brother Roland Stocks on 4/11/12 at $31.50 a share how much money did your money make with a .41 cent dividend?

$$1,000 \times .41 = \$ 410.00 \text{ dollars}$$
$$1,000 \times 1.10 = \$1,100.00 \text{ dollars}$$

You made a total of $1,510.00 dollars in 30 days. You might be saying to yourself, that's too good to be true? What if the stock went down $1.10 instead of up $1.10? If you keep the stocks it will make money for you as long as you don't sell them below the price you bought them at. Now what if you knew that the price of the stock was going to go up $6.00 dollars or more, but you didn't know when? Which is why you bought this stock in the first place.

How much money would you have made if you bought 10,000 shares?

$$\$1,510.00 \times 10 = \$15,100.00 \text{ dollars}$$

What if you sold after it went up $3.00 dollars more, how much money would your money have made for you?

$$\$ 15,100.00 \times 3 = \$45, 300.00 \text{ dollars}$$

Is this starting to look more like retirement to you? How about after three or more trades just like this one did? This is another page you might put on your favorites list. If you start off with a small amount of money, chances are you will be making small amounts of money. The more money you have to trade with, the more you will make. Your next chapter will show you which stocks will move faster than others, so your money isn't tied up for a long time.

Let's have a look, shall we?

## CHAPTER FOUR

# You want to find stocks that move faster

Y our next criteria is to separate the slow moving stocks from the fast moving stocks, so you can get your money to make more money faster. The more up and down a stock moves in one trading day in let's say 40 days; the faster your money can make money for you. Just think about the ocean and how it constantly moves up and down. Every stock you own or trade with should do the same thing. You're going to find stocks that move more than others, because if the water is stagnant or not going up or down in just a little bit of time it begins to stink and so will you trade.

Let's look at the example I have
for you on the next page, shall we?

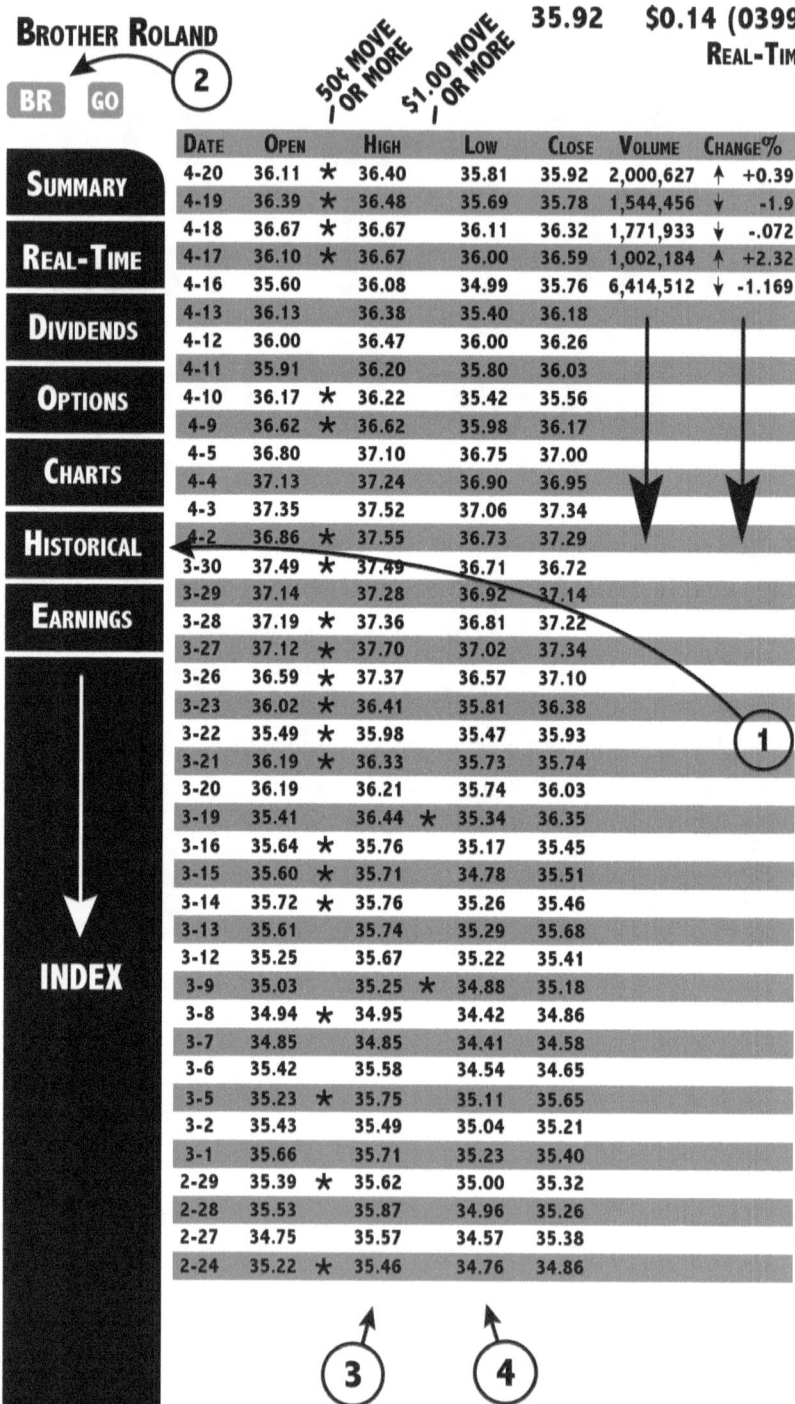

**Brother Roland**

BR  GO  (2)

50¢ MOVE / OR MORE

$1.00 MOVE / OR MORE

35.92  $0.14 (0399)
REAL-TIME

| | | | | | | | |
|---|---|---|---|---|---|---|---|
| SUMMARY | REAL-TIME | DIVIDENDS | OPTIONS | CHARTS | HISTORICAL | EARNINGS | INDEX |

| DATE | OPEN | | HIGH | LOW | | CLOSE | VOLUME | CHANGE% |
|---|---|---|---|---|---|---|---|---|
| 4-20 | 36.11 | ★ | 36.40 | 35.81 | | 35.92 | 2,000,627 | ↑ +0.39 |
| 4-19 | 36.39 | ★ | 36.48 | 35.69 | | 35.78 | 1,544,456 | ↓ -1.9 |
| 4-18 | 36.67 | ★ | 36.67 | 36.11 | | 36.32 | 1,771,933 | ↓ -.072 |
| 4-17 | 36.10 | ★ | 36.67 | 36.00 | | 36.59 | 1,002,184 | ↑ +2.32 |
| 4-16 | 35.60 | | 36.08 | 34.99 | | 35.76 | 6,414,512 | ↓ -1.169 |
| 4-13 | 36.13 | | 36.38 | 35.40 | | 36.18 | | |
| 4-12 | 36.00 | | 36.47 | 36.00 | | 36.26 | | |
| 4-11 | 35.91 | | 36.20 | 35.80 | | 36.03 | | |
| 4-10 | 36.17 | ★ | 36.22 | 35.42 | | 35.56 | | |
| 4-9 | 36.62 | ★ | 36.62 | 35.98 | | 36.17 | | |
| 4-5 | 36.80 | | 37.10 | 36.75 | | 37.00 | | |
| 4-4 | 37.13 | | 37.24 | 36.90 | | 36.95 | | |
| 4-3 | 37.35 | | 37.52 | 37.06 | | 37.34 | | |
| 4-2 | 36.86 | ★ | 37.55 | 36.73 | | 37.29 | | |
| 3-30 | 37.49 | ★ | 37.49 | 36.71 | | 36.72 | | |
| 3-29 | 37.14 | | 37.28 | 36.92 | | 37.14 | | |
| 3-28 | 37.19 | ★ | 37.36 | 36.81 | | 37.22 | | |
| 3-27 | 37.12 | ★ | 37.70 | 37.02 | | 37.34 | | |
| 3-26 | 36.59 | ★ | 37.37 | 36.57 | | 37.10 | | |
| 3-23 | 36.02 | ★ | 36.41 | 35.81 | | 36.38 | | |
| 3-22 | 35.49 | ★ | 35.98 | 35.47 | | 35.93 | | |
| 3-21 | 36.19 | ★ | 36.33 | 35.73 | | 35.74 | | |
| 3-20 | 36.19 | | 36.21 | 35.74 | | 36.03 | | |
| 3-19 | 35.41 | | 36.44 | ★ 35.34 | | 36.35 | | |
| 3-16 | 35.64 | ★ | 35.76 | 35.17 | | 35.45 | | |
| 3-15 | 35.60 | ★ | 35.71 | 34.78 | | 35.51 | | |
| 3-14 | 35.72 | ★ | 35.76 | 35.26 | | 35.46 | | |
| 3-13 | 35.61 | | 35.74 | 35.29 | | 35.68 | | |
| 3-12 | 35.25 | | 35.67 | 35.22 | | 35.41 | | |
| 3-9 | 35.03 | | 35.25 | ★ 34.88 | | 35.18 | | |
| 3-8 | 34.94 | ★ | 34.95 | 34.42 | | 34.86 | | |
| 3-7 | 34.85 | | 34.85 | 34.41 | | 34.58 | | |
| 3-6 | 35.42 | | 35.58 | 34.54 | | 34.65 | | |
| 3-5 | 35.23 | ★ | 35.75 | 35.11 | | 35.65 | | |
| 3-2 | 35.43 | | 35.49 | 35.04 | | 35.21 | | |
| 3-1 | 35.66 | | 35.71 | 35.23 | | 35.40 | | |
| 2-29 | 35.39 | ★ | 35.62 | 35.00 | | 35.32 | | |
| 2-28 | 35.53 | | 35.87 | 34.96 | | 35.26 | | |
| 2-27 | 34.75 | | 35.57 | 34.57 | | 35.38 | | |
| 2-24 | 35.22 | ★ | 35.46 | 34.76 | | 34.86 | | |

(1)

(3)

(4)

Once you go on to your favorite's page that has a graph on it or your brokerage firms summary page and put in the stock symbol or name and go there, then just click on . . .

1) Historical prices. If you look at example #1

2) Tells us that the stock name is Brother Roland (BR).

3) Indicates how many times the stock went up and down more than .50 cents.

4) Indicates how many times the stock went up and down more than 1.00 dollar.

In order to get these *; you need to look at the high and low on each date and determine which date did what. I put a * in place whenever the stock made .50 cents or more; between column two and three and I put a * every time the stock made over $1.00 dollar between column three and four. I have made three examples for you to examine or look over carefully. Each example shows stocks that are close to the same price range. There are seven or more different columns going across the page.

Column . . .

1) What the stock did on that date.

2) What price the stock started or opened at.

3) Tells us the highest price that the stock did all day

4) Tells us the lowest price that the stock did all day.

5) Tells us where the stock closed at.

6) Tells us how many trades the stock was bought or sold throughout the day.

7) Tells us the difference the stock did in a % from one day to the next.

The * lets us know what the stock did and how often. In 40 days (BR) moved .50 cents or more 23 times and $1.00 or more 2 times.

Now let's look at #2 stock example, shall we?

As you can see here, this stock only moved .50 cents or more two times out of 40. Although this stock had great dividends in payout; and has been around for a long time: it does not have much up and down movement. This is what I call stagnant water and it stinks. This stock is a good stock to buy for the dividend payouts on a long term plan, but it should not be used on a large buy or trade.

* Lesson to learn here. *

I played a slow moving stock like this one and made $1,500.00 dollars on the dividend payout. But, because the stock lost $1.00.00 dollar in value; I held on to those stocks because, the $100, 000.00 dollars I bought the stock with would have lost me $8,500.00 dollars if I sold them right after the dividend paid out. I sold them right after I made my money back, because I knew where the stock was going. It kept me holding on to those stocks for four months before I could sell them. Needless to say, It seem to take for ever for that stock to turn around and make money for me. That's why you want a fast moving stock. Don't make the same mistake I did.

# BROTHER ROLAND

BR GO

50¢ MOVE
/ OR MORE

SUMMARY

REAL-TIME

DIVIDENDS

OPTIONS

CHARTS

HISTORICAL

EARNINGS

↓

INDEX

#2
ex.

| DATE | OPEN | HIGH | LOW | CLOSE |
|------|------|------|-----|-------|
| 4-20 | 30.74 | 31.09 | 30.70 | 30.86 |
| 4-19 | 30.78 | 30.88 | 30.60 | 30.74 |
| 4-18 | 30.75 | 30.85 | 30.66 | 30.75 |
| 4-17 | 30.77 | 30.95 | 30.67 | 30.89 |
| 4-16 | 30.56 | 30.72 | 30.50 | 30.61 |
| 4-13 | 30.75 | 30.86 | 30.52 | 30.54 |
| 4-12 | 30.79 | 30.88 | 30.68 | 30.84 |
| 4-11 | 30.39 | 30.51 | 30.27 | 30.45 |
| 4-10 | 30.52 | 30.62 ★ | 29.95 | 30.13 |
| 4-9 | 30.70 | 30.84 | 30.55 | 30.64 |
| 4-5 | 31.09 | 31.16 | 30.75 | 30.94 |
| 4-4 | 31.40 | 31.66 | 31.38 | 31.57 |
| 4-3 | 31.46 | 31.60 | 31.33 | 31.43 |
| 4-2 | 31.33 | 31.59 | 31.27 | 31.45 |
| 3-30 | 31.32 | 31.38 | 31.16 | 31.23 |
| 3-29 | 31.05 | 31.21 | 30.27 | 31.21 |
| 3-28 | 31.53 | 31.57 | 31.20 | 31.36 |
| 3-27 | 31.79 | 31.95 | 31.60 | 31.64 |
| 3-26 | 31.61 | 31.83 | 31.59 | 31.79 |
| 3-23 | 31.64 | 31.72 | 31.38 | 31.52 |
| 3-22 | 31.76 | 31.86 | 31.56 | 31.71 |
| 3-21 | 31.85 | 31.97 | 31.83 | 31.84 |
| 3-20 | 31.60 | 31.83 | 31.51 | 31.79 |
| 3-19 | 31.44 | 31.74 | 31.35 | 31.65 |
| 3-16 | 31.70 | 31.71 | 31.51 | 31.59 |
| 3-15 | 31.41 | 31.65 | 31.35 | 31.64 |
| 3-14 | 31.60 | 31.80 | 31.42 | 31.45 |
| 3-13 | 31.49 | 31.64 | 31.44 | 31.63 |
| 3-12 | 31.20 | 31.52 | 31.18 | 31.44 |
| 3-9 | 31.00 | 31.18 | 31.00 | 31.18 |
| 3-8 | 31.09 | 31.15 | 30.88 | 31.00 |
| 3-7 | 30.69 | 30.97 | 30.69 | 30.88 |
| 3-6 | 30.80 | 30.97 | 30.66 | 30.72 |
| 3-5 | 30.85 | 31.12 | 30.75 | 30.99 |
| 3-2 | 30.67 | 31.00 | 30.60 | 30.87 |
| 3-1 | 30.54 | 30.66 ★ | 30.15 | 30.63 |
| 2-29 | 30.47 | 30.64 | 30.47 | 30.59 |
| 2-28 | 30.41 | 30.58 | 30.36 | 30.53 |
| 2-27 | 30.31 | 30.43 | 30.29 | 30.36 |
| 2-24 | 30.40 | 30.49 | 30.29 | 30.34 |

# BROTHER ROLAND

32.06 ↑ $0.30

BR GO

SUMMARY

REAL-TIME

DIVIDENDS

OPTIONS

CHARTS

HISTORICAL

EARNINGS

↓

INDEX

#3
ex.

50¢ MOVE OR MORE

$2.00 MOVE OR MORE

| DATE | OPEN | | HIGH | LOW | | CLOSE |
|------|------|---|------|-----|---|-------|
| 4-20 | 31.95 | ★ | 32.44 | 31.76 | | 32.06 |
| 4-19 | 32.06 | ★ | 32.35 | 31.74 | | 31.76 |
| 4-18 | 31.77 | ★ | 32.41 | 31.67 | | 32.11 |
| 4-17 | 31.40 | ★ | 31.88 | 31.18 | | 31.80 |
| 4-16 | 31.43 | | 32.67 | 30.54 | ★ | 31.01 |
| 4-13 | 34.17 | | 34.34 | 33.96 | | 34.13 |
| 4-12 | 33.85 | ★ | 34.50 | 33.76 | | 34.30 |
| 4-11 | 33.24 | ★ | 33.75 | 33.08 | | 33.68 |
| 4-10 | 33.42 | ★ | 33.75 | 32.94 | | 33.00 |
| 4-9 | 33.46 | | 33.73 | 33.25 | | 33.64 |
| 4-5 | 33.67 | | 34.07 | 33.67 | | 33.92 |
| 4-4 | 34.01 | ★ | 34.25 | 33.83 | | 33.88 |
| 4-3 | 34.14 | ★ | 34.56 | 34.05 | | 34.24 |
| 4-2 | 33.62 | ★ | 34.23 | 33.62 | | 34.13 |
| 3-30 | 34.22 | ★ | 34.37 | 33.64 | | 33.66 |
| 3-29 | 33.94 | | 34.07 | 33.66 | | 34.03 |
| 3-28 | 34.45 | ★ | 34.45 | 33.83 | | 34.10 |
| 3-27 | 34.55 | | 34.62 | 34.24 | | 34.38 |
| 3-26 | 34.00 | ★ | 34.48 | 33.81 | | 34.38 |
| 3-23 | 33.61 | ★ | 33.82 | 33.27 | | 33.76 |
| 3-22 | 33.03 | ★ | 33.70 | 33.03 | | 33.64 |
| 3-21 | 33.55 | | 33.55 | 33.30 | | 33.32 |
| 3-20 | 33.28 | | 33.62 | 33.25 | | 33.50 |
| 3-19 | 33.39 | ★ | 33.70 | 33.00 | | 33.53 |
| 3-16 | 33.36 | | 33.46 | 32.97 | | 33.06 |
| 3-15 | 33.43 | | 33.48 | 33.04 | | 33.36 |
| 3-14 | 33.50 | | 33.58 | 33.31 | | 33.42 |
| 3-13 | 33.65 | | 33.65 | 33.25 | | 33.53 |
| 3-12 | 33.43 | | 33.54 | 33.28 | | 33.39 |
| 3-9 | 33.06 | | 33.40 | 32.97 | | 33.39 |
| 3-8 | 32.97 | ★ | 33.16 | 32.62 | | 33.06 |
| 3-7 | 32.28 | | 32.56 | 32.19 | | 32.50 |
| 3-6 | 32.80 | | 33.13 | 32.21 | | 32.23 |
| 3-5 | 32.68 | ★ | 33.10 | 32.60 | | 33.03 |
| 3-2 | 32.86 | ★ | 32.89 | 32.40 | | 32.68 |
| 3-1 | 32.62 | | 32.95 | 32.47 | | 32.82 |
| 2-29 | 32.63 | | 32.70 | 32.43 | | 32.44 |
| 2-28 | 32.34 | | 32.69 | 32.29 | | 32.59 |
| 2-27 | 31.89 | ★ | 32.47 | 31.84 | | 32.33 |
| 2-24 | 32.39 | | 32.39 | 32.07 | | 32.16 |

( 20 ) TIMES          ( 1 ) TIME

Let's look at example #3, shall we?

Notice how the .50 cent or more moved 21 times out of 40. And $2.00.00 dollars or more one time. Examples #I and #3 are what you are looking for. They both have been around more than ten years, they both have great dividend payouts, and they both moved $.50 cent more than half the time it is being traded. Because they both hit these three criteria's; they and any others like them are what you want in your portfolio.

Now just because you may not have the money to get started in trades, yet. It does not mean you don't have time to find 20 or more stocks that meat these same criteria's These are the same stocks I buy for my 10% portfolio page. This will also save you a lot of time whenever you want to see how they are doing.

I recommend if you don't have money to trade with, make all of your trades on paper and see if you would have made money on your trades? This way when you do have money to make real trades with, you will be ready to do so. Until you get a good sizeable portfolio and enough money to make money for you; it's best you spend time with your charts.

That's where Chapter Five comes in.

# CHAPTER FIVE

# You next move is to put together your portfolio

The next nine pages will show you what you will need to put together on each stock you have. In order to have a working portfolio that works for you, each stock must fall into all of the criteria's we talked about so far. The more money you want your money to make for you will come down to how many good stock you have to choose from in your portfolio.

You first want to look at what your stock did from day one until today. If you look on the next page you will see that in order to get this chart you must click on MAX on the strip below the graph. This graph tells you, where your stock came from and it's been around for 27 years and was at $35.92 dollars 15 minutes ago. You will find out, that the more information you have on your stock the more time you will save when you want to know where it will go.

Because the highest point on the graph shows that it was within the last three years from today; you want to make a copy of the five year graph, like the one on page 43.

Let's have a look, shall we?

41

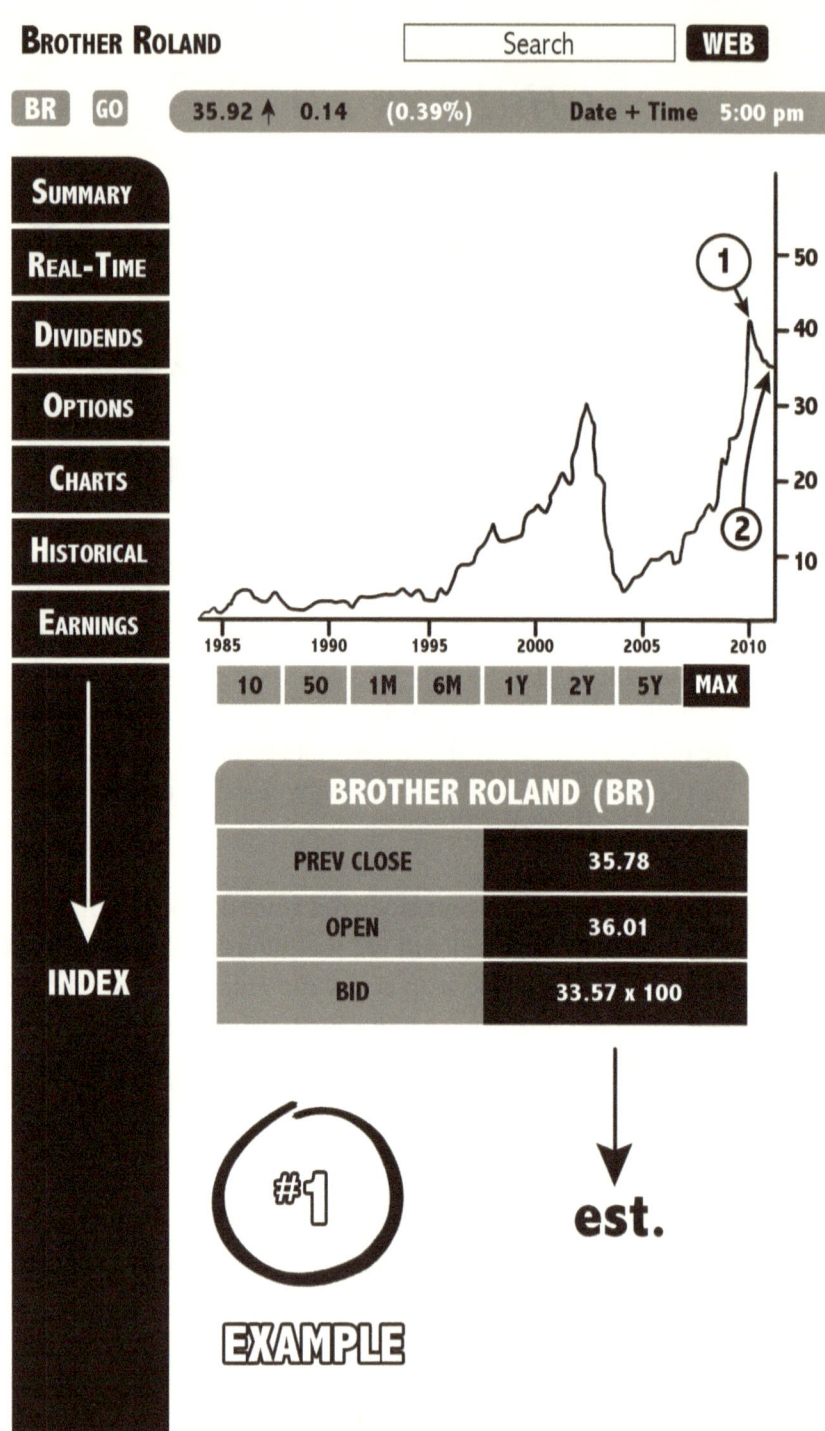

BROTHER ROLAND

Search | WEB

BR GO | 35.92 ↑ 0.14 (0.39%) | Date + Time 5:00 pm

SUMMARY

REAL-TIME

DIVIDENDS

OPTIONS

CHARTS

HISTORICAL

EARNINGS

INDEX

**BROTHER ROLAND (BR)**

| PREV CLOSE | 35.78 |
|---|---|
| OPEN | 36.01 |
| BID | 33.57 x 100 |

#1

EXAMPLE

est.

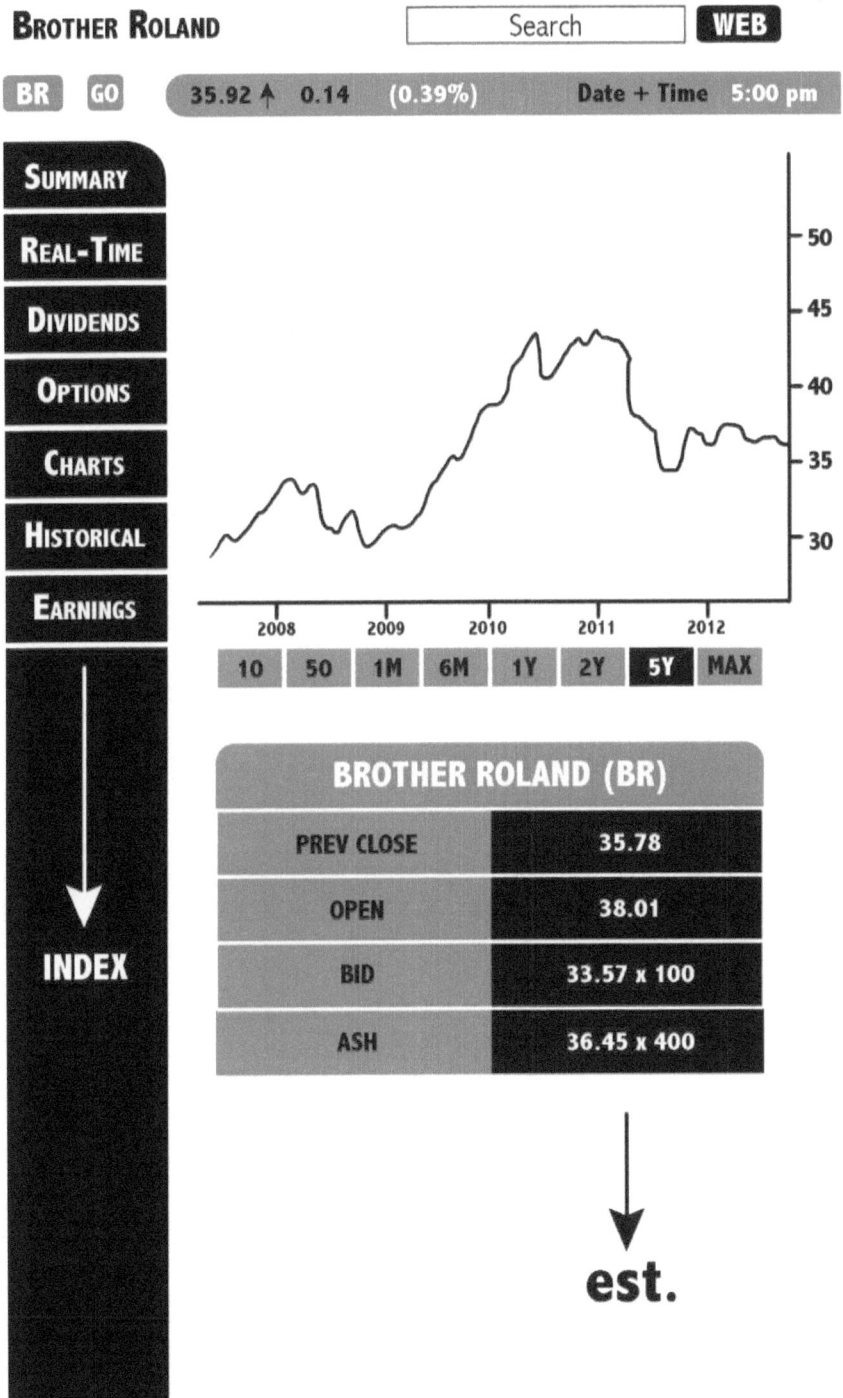

BROTHER ROLAND

Search    WEB

BR   GO    35.92 ↑ 0.14    (0.39%)    Date + Time   5:00 pm

- SUMMARY
- REAL-TIME
- DIVIDENDS
- OPTIONS
- CHARTS
- HISTORICAL
- EARNINGS

INDEX

| 10 | 50 | 1M | 6M | 1Y | 2Y | 5Y | MAX |

| BROTHER ROLAND (BR) | |
|---|---|
| PREV CLOSE | 35.78 |
| OPEN | 38.01 |
| BID | 33.57 x 100 |
| ASH | 36.45 x 400 |

est.

Now that you know where your stock came from you will want a copy of the one year graph to tell you where it's going.

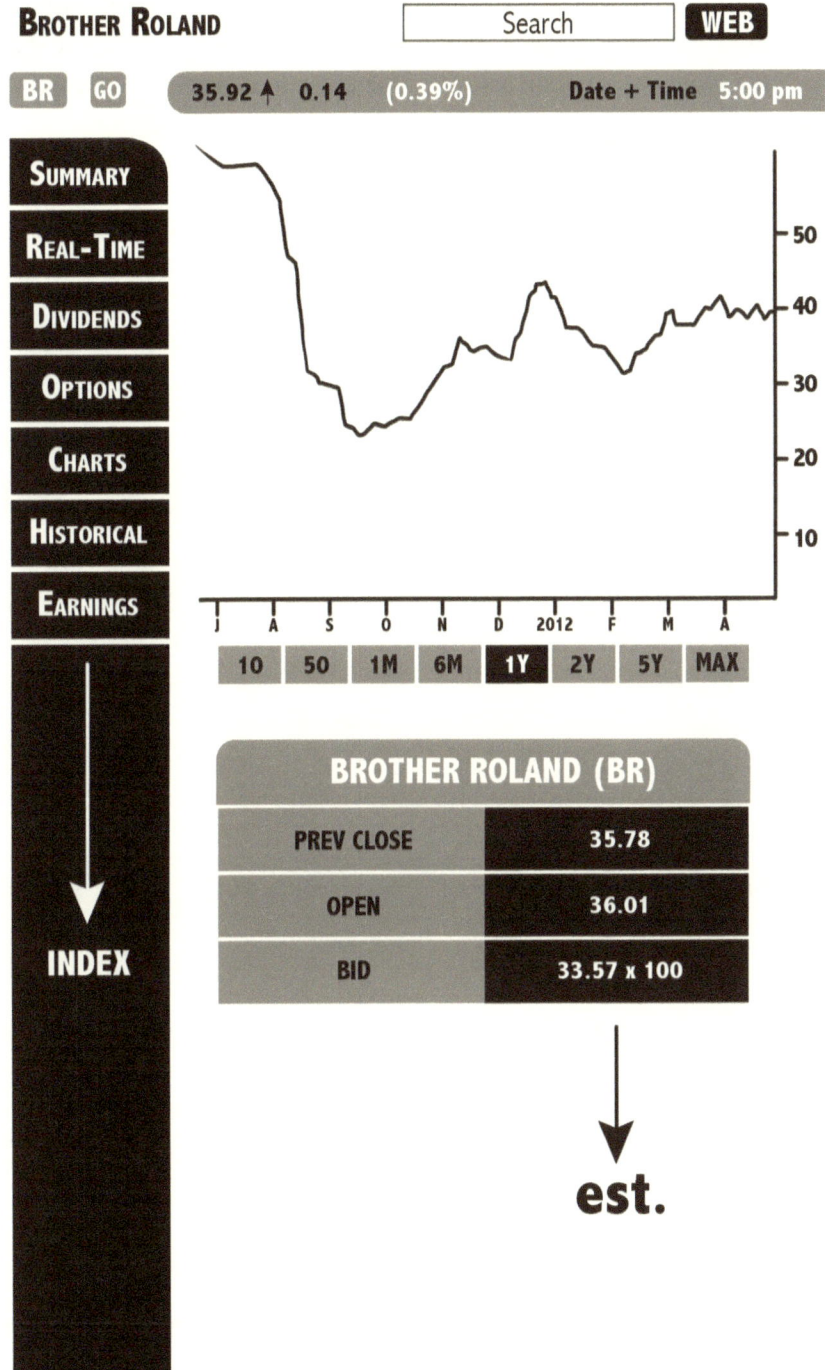

**BROTHER ROLAND**

Search  WEB

BR  GO   35.92 ↑ 0.14   (0.39%)      Date + Time   5:00 pm

SUMMARY

REAL-TIME

DIVIDENDS

OPTIONS

CHARTS

HISTORICAL

EARNINGS

INDEX

J  A  S  O  N  D  2012  F  M  A

10  50  1M  6M  1Y  2Y  5Y  MAX

50
40
30
20
10

| BROTHER ROLAND (BR) | |
| --- | --- |
| PREV CLOSE | 35.78 |
| OPEN | 36.01 |
| BID | 33.57 x 100 |

est.

It's also important to know the history about your stock and it will tell you how many times your stock moved more than .50 cents in one day on a 40 day chart. You can also use this chart to compare it to another stock.

SUMMARY
REAL-TIME
DIVIDENDS
OPTIONS
CHARTS
HISTORICAL
EARNINGS

INDEX

| Date | Open | High | Low | Close | Volume | Change% |
|------|------|------|-----|-------|--------|---------|
| 4-20 | 36.11 ★ | 36.40 | 35.81 | 35.92 | 2,000,627 | ↑ +0.39 |
| 4-19 | 36.39 ★ | 36.48 | 35.69 | 35.78 | 1,544,456 | ↓ -1.9 |
| 4-18 | 36.67 ★ | 36.67 | 36.11 | 36.32 | 1,771,933 | ↓ -.072 |
| 4-17 | 36.10 ★ | 36.67 | 36.00 | 36.59 | 1,002,184 | ↑ +2.32 |
| 4-16 | 35.60 | 36.08 | 34.99 | 35.76 | 6,414,512 | ↓ -1.169 |
| 4-13 | 36.13 | 36.38 | 35.40 | 36.18 | | |
| 4-12 | 36.00 | 36.47 | 36.00 | 36.26 | | |
| 4-11 | 35.91 | 36.20 | 35.80 | 36.03 | | |
| 4-10 | 36.17 ★ | 36.22 | 35.42 | 35.56 | | |
| 4-9 | 36.62 ★ | 36.62 | 35.98 | 36.17 | | |
| 4-5 | 36.80 | 37.10 | 36.75 | 37.00 | | |
| 4-4 | 37.13 | 37.24 | 36.90 | 36.95 | | |
| 4-3 | 37.35 | 37.52 | 37.06 | 37.34 | | |
| 4-2 | 36.86 ★ | 37.55 | 36.73 | 37.29 | | |
| 3-30 | 37.49 ★ | 37.49 | 36.71 | 36.72 | | |
| 3-29 | 37.14 | 37.28 | 36.92 | 37.14 | | |
| 3-28 | 37.19 ★ | 37.36 | 36.81 | 37.22 | | |
| 3-27 | 37.12 ★ | 37.70 | 37.02 | 37.34 | | |
| 3-26 | 36.59 ★ | 37.37 | 36.57 | 37.10 | | |
| 3-23 | 36.02 ★ | 36.41 | 35.81 | 36.38 | | |
| 3-22 | 35.49 ★ | 35.98 | 35.47 | 35.93 | | |
| 3-21 | 36.19 ★ | 36.33 | 35.73 | 35.74 | | |
| 3-20 | 36.19 | 36.21 | 35.74 | 36.03 | | |
| 3-19 | 35.41 | 36.44 ★ | 35.34 | 36.35 | | |
| 3-16 | 35.64 ★ | 35.76 | 35.17 | 35.45 | | |
| 3-15 | 35.60 ★ | 35.71 | 34.78 | 35.51 | | |
| 3-14 | 35.72 ★ | 35.76 | 35.26 | 35.46 | | |
| 3-13 | 35.61 | 35.74 | 35.29 | 35.68 | | |
| 3-12 | 35.25 | 35.67 | 35.22 | 35.41 | | |
| 3-9 | 35.03 | 35.25 ★ | 34.88 | 35.18 | | |
| 3-8 | 34.94 ★ | 34.95 | 34.42 | 34.86 | | |
| 3-7 | 34.85 | 34.85 | 34.41 | 34.58 | | |
| 3-6 | 35.42 | 35.58 | 34.54 | 34.65 | | |
| 3-5 | 35.23 ★ | 35.75 | 35.11 | 35.65 | | |
| 3-2 | 35.43 | 35.49 | 35.04 | 35.21 | | |
| 3-1 | 35.66 | 35.71 | 35.23 | 35.40 | | |
| 2-29 | 35.39 ★ | 35.62 | 35.00 | 35.32 | | |
| 2-28 | 35.53 | 35.87 | 34.96 | 35.26 | | |
| 2-27 | 34.75 | 35.57 | 34.57 | 35.38 | | |
| 2-24 | 35.22 ★ | 35.46 | 34.76 | 34.86 | | |

BR  GO

# DIVIDEND HISTORY

SUMMARY

REAL-TIME

DIVIDENDS

OPTIONS

CHARTS

HISTORICAL

EARNINGS

INDEX

| PAYABLE | AMOUNT/SHARE | EX-DATE |
| --- | --- | --- |
| 11-15-2011 | $0.30 | 10-28-2011 |
| 8-15-2011 | $0.30 | 7-28-2011 |
| 5-16-2011 | $0.30 | 4-28-2011 |
| 2-15-2011 | $0.25 | 1-28-2011 |
| 11-15-2010 | $0.25 | 10-28-2010 |
| 8-15-2010 | $0.25 | 7-29-2010 |
| 5-15-2010 | $0.25 | 4-29-2010 |
| 2-15-2010 | $0.20 | 1-29-2010 |
| 11-15-2009 | $0.20 | 10-29-2009 |
| 8-15-2009 | $0.20 | 7-30-2009 |
| 5-15-2009 | $0.20 | 4-29-2009 |
| 2-15-2009 | $0.20 | 1-30-2009 |
| 11-15-2008 | $0.20 | 10-30-2008 |
| 8-15-2008 | $0.20 | 7-30-2008 |
| 5-15-2008 | $0.20 | 4-30-2008 |
| 2-15-2008 | $0.16 | 1-30-2008 |
| 11-15-2007 | $0.16 | 10-30-2007 |
| 8-15-2007 | $0.16 | 7-30-2007 |
| 5-15-2007 | $0.16 | 4-27-2007 |

It's also good to know when your stock is giving out any dividends or payout. You should look for around 20 stocks to put into your own portfolio that meet all the criteria's. Keep all of your other stocks information in some other folder. Now you are ready for the last criteria.

Let's have a look, shall we?

# CHAPTER SIX

# When to buy; and when to sell

T his last criteria is the most important one to know; because it tells you where the stock will go, as well as when to get in and when to get out.

Two years before I retired, I worked for a good company for 18 years and never missed a day's work. My 401k at the time only had $62,000.00 dollar and I just got done paying off my truck loan. You see I was paying 6% interest to myself buy taking a loan against my 401k money. The markets were not doing too good at that time so I took out a new loan for my mortgage for the place I was living in. This way I could pay myself 6% back on my own loan or mortgage. Because the markets were so bad and I just lost over 40% of my 401k. Through no fault of my own, the brokerage firm that my company had my 401k account in did not know what I was about to find out.

Let's have a look, shall we?

Then I noticed something when I looked at my companies stock and it was selling at $3.50 dollars a share and normally it's been at $15.00 dollars at average for the 18 years that I worked for them. So I took the last $18,000.00 dollars I had in my 401k money market fund and went all in on my companies stock. The year before this stock had hit an all-time high of $48.00 dollars a share; I figured that I would keep my money in until it got close to its 50% mark which was $24.00 dollars a share. Nine months later I got out at $22.00 dollars a share. My portfolio went from $62,000.00 dollars to $120,000.00 dollars.

The stock went up to $26.00 dollars or $28.00 dollars a share. If I kept my money in longer, I could have made more money.

Then the stock started going back down and down and down. My 401k brokerage firm would not let me buy that stock until 90 days had passed. My 401k would only allow me to trade or move my money around three times in one year; after 90 days I got bake in at $14.50 dollars a share with $80,000.00 dollars and got out at the 50% mark and my portfolio had $225.000.00 dollars in it. The stock went up to $24.00 or $26.00 dollars a share and then started going back down.

Again I could not buy until 90 days had gone by; although the stock went down to $15.00 dollars a share, I got in at $17.00 dollars a share and when it got to $21.00 dollars a share I told my boss when the stock hits $22.00 dollars a share I would give them my two weeks' notice. Needless to say, that vary next day I handed them my notice and walked away with over $300.000.00 dollars in my account and never looked back.

You were right when you asked yourself, Could I go into retirement on only one stock? Just imagine what you could have done with four or five more stocks just like this one? Instead of weighting 90 days for your money to get back in, you could have played one of the other stocks in your portfolio. All of the criteria's were in the stock that I used to trade with.

1) The stock was a company that was around for over 10 years.

2) The stock moved more than .50 cents in half the times of 30 days.

3) The stock also paid out dividends.

4) The last criteria, was the 50% mark or line.

So let's look at the example on the next page, shall we?

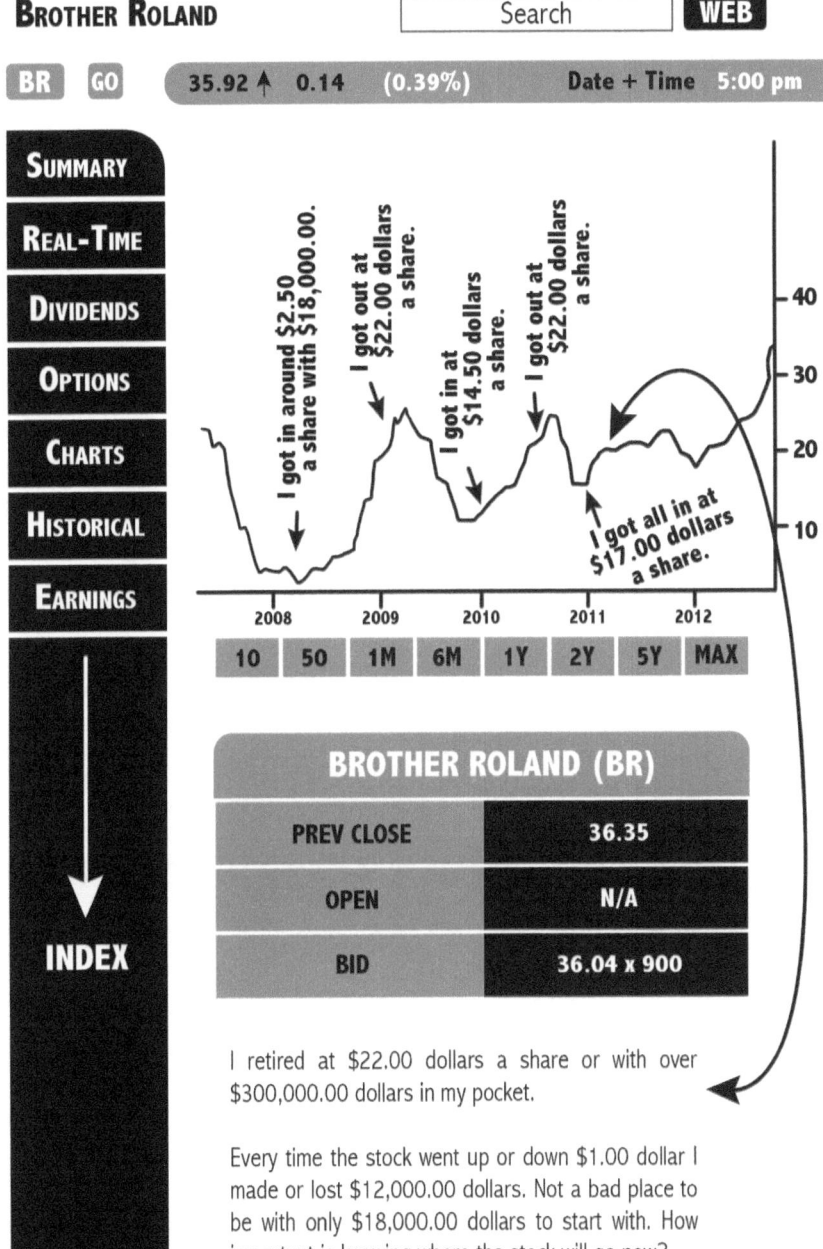

Search    **WEB**

BR  GO    35.92 ↑  0.14    (0.39%)    Date + Time    5:00 pm

SUMMARY

REAL-TIME

DIVIDENDS

OPTIONS

CHARTS

HISTORICAL

EARNINGS

INDEX

I got in around $2.50 a share with $18,000.00.

I got out at $22.00 dollars a share.

I got in at $14.50 dollars a share.

I got out at $22.00 dollars a share.

I got all in at $17.00 dollars a share.

40
30
20
10

2008    2009    2010    2011    2012

10  50  1M  6M  1Y  2Y  5Y  MAX

| BROTHER ROLAND (BR) | |
|---|---|
| PREV CLOSE | 36.35 |
| OPEN | N/A |
| BID | 36.04 x 900 |

I retired at $22.00 dollars a share or with over $300,000.00 dollars in my pocket.

Every time the stock went up or down $1.00 dollar I made or lost $12,000.00 dollars. Not a bad place to be with only $18,000.00 dollars to start with. How important is knowing where the stock will go now?

This # 1 example shows us what Brother Roland (BR) did for over 27 years. When you want to find a 50% line or mark, you have to find the highest point that the stock did, marked # (1) on your graph and the lowest point to the right of that highest point marked # (2.) What we are looking for is a 50% line or place that has not yet been hit.

Because we can get a better reading
on our 5 year graph lets go there, shall we?

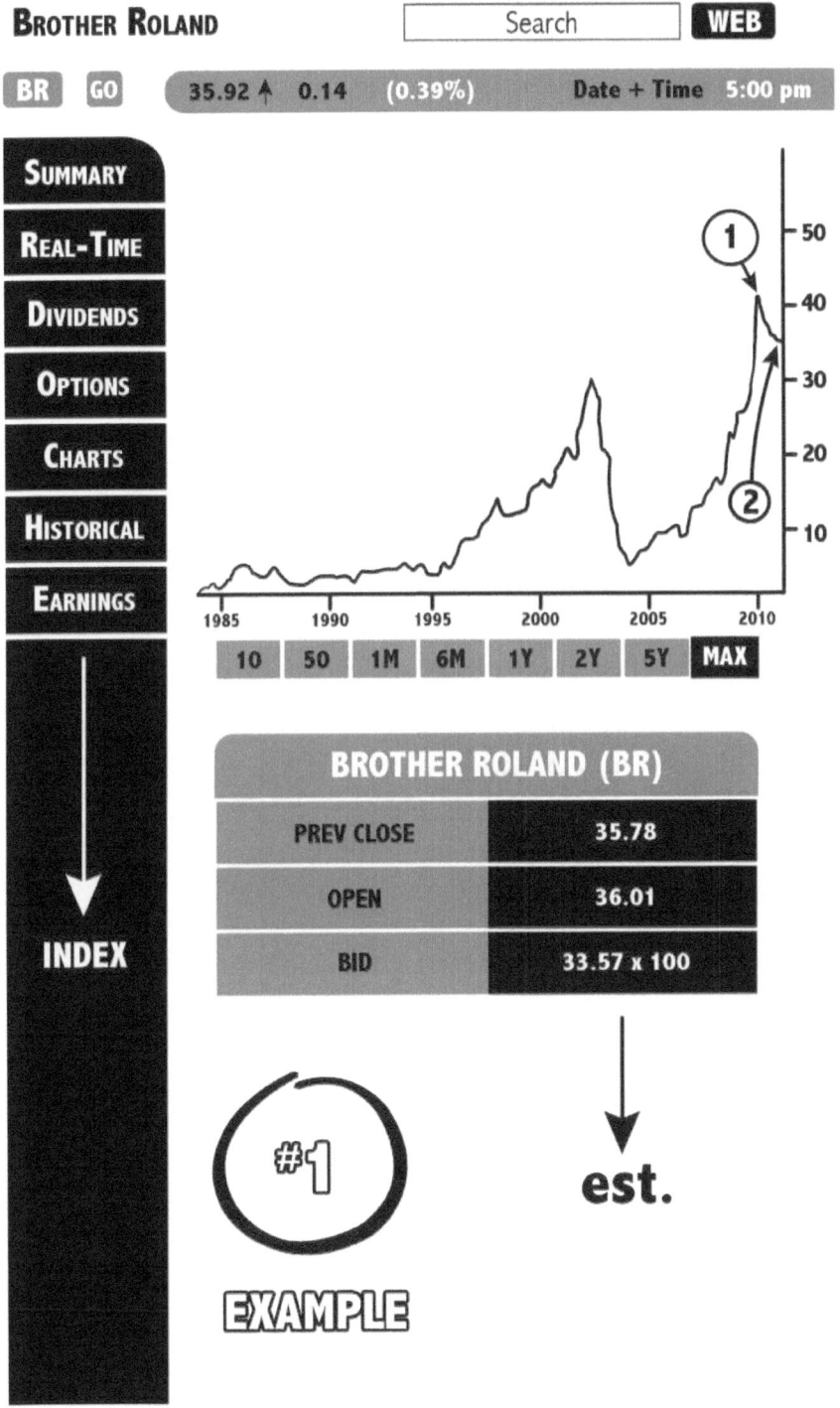

This # 2 example shows us what Brother Roland (BR) did for the last five years. # (1) spot on this graph is the highest point on the graph, but is it the highest point without hitting a 50% line or mark?

Let's look, shall we?

The high on point # (1) = $49.65
The low on point # (2) = $43.91
$49.65 + $43.91 = $93.56 / 2 = $46.78 /50%

Point # (3) is our next new high because the 50% line was hit by it.

The new high on point # (3) = $48.05
The new low on point # (4) = $42.67
$48.05 + $42.67 = $90.72 / 2 = $45.36 /50%

Point # (5) is $45.26 which did not hit the 50% line. So that makes point # (6) your new low.

The new high on point # (3) = $48.05
The new low on point # (6) = $31.89
$48.05 + $31.89 = $79.94 / 2 = $39.97 /50%

Our new 50% line is $39.97, but is this the real 50% line.

Let's look at what our one year graph looks like, shall we?

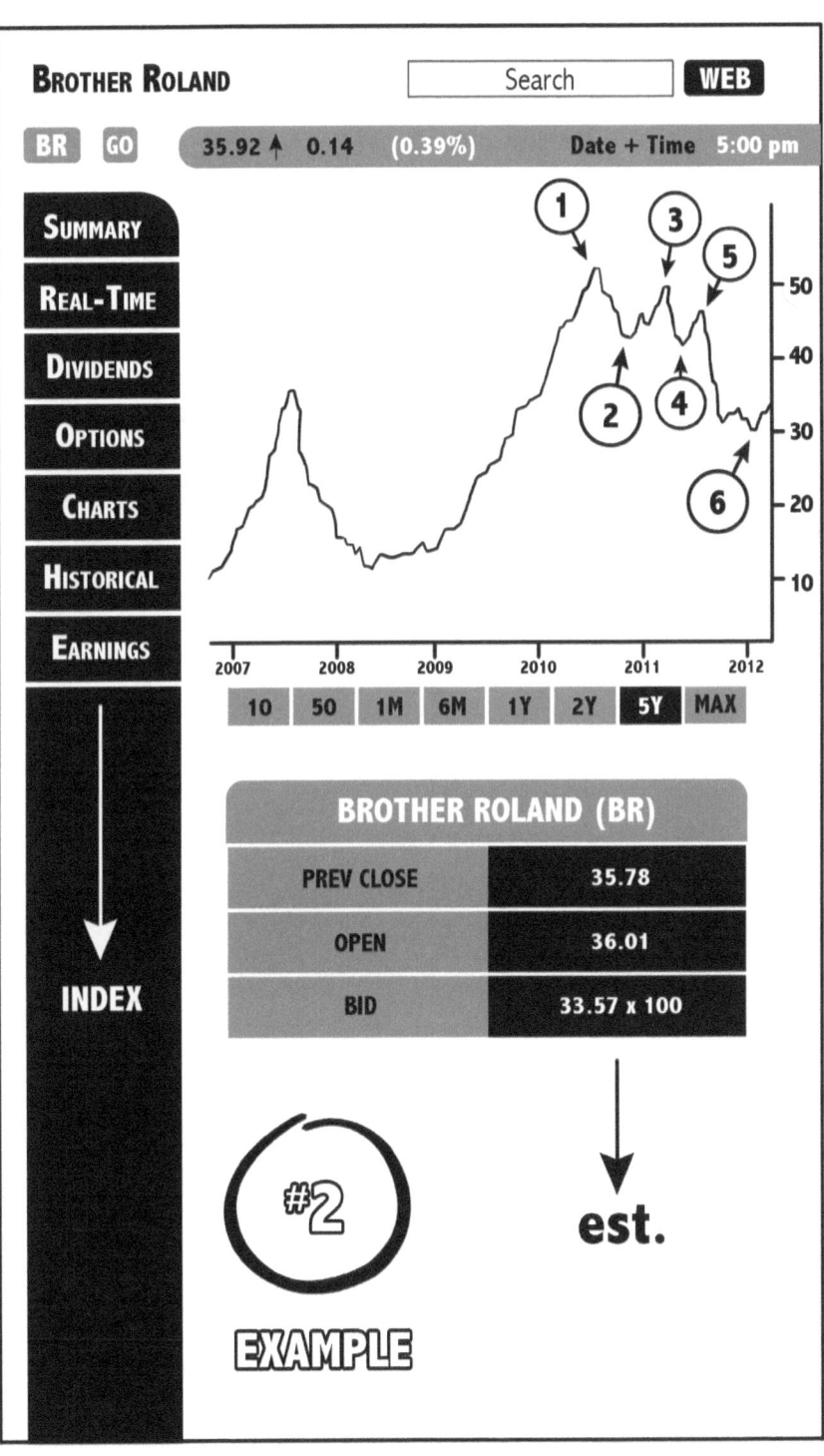

This # 3 example shows us what Brother Roland (BR) did in one year.

The high on point # (1) = $47.97
The low on point # (2) = $42.67
$47.97 + $42.67 = $90.64 / 2 = $45.32 /50%

Point # (3) is our next new high because the 50% line was hit by it.

The new high on point # (3) = $45.86
The new low on point # (4) = $31.99
$45.86 + $31.99 = $87.85 / 2 = $38.92 /50%

The 50% line was not hit on point # (4) and because point # (5) is lower than point # (4) that makes point # (5) your new low.

The new high on point # (3) = $45.86
The new low on point # (5) = $31.65
$45.86 + $31.65 = $77.51 / 2 = $38.75 /50%

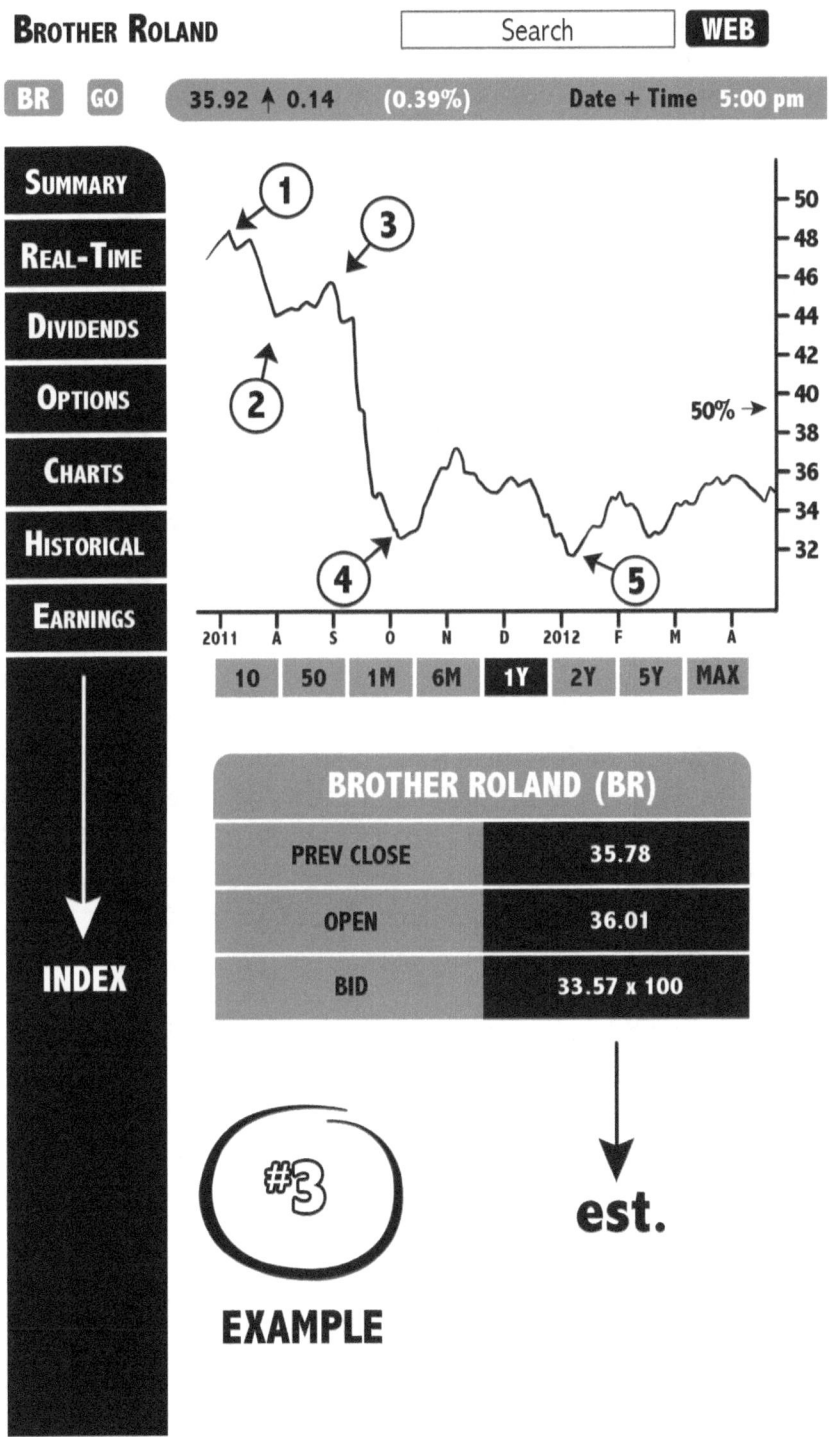

BROTHER ROLAND

Search    WEB

BR  GO    35.92 ↑ 0.14    (0.39%)    Date + Time   5:00 pm

SUMMARY

REAL-TIME

DIVIDENDS

OPTIONS

CHARTS

HISTORICAL

EARNINGS

INDEX

2011  A  S  O  N  D  2012  F  M  A

50%→

— 50
— 48
— 46
— 44
— 42
— 40
— 38
— 36
— 34
— 32

10  50  1M  6M  1Y  2Y  5Y  MAX

| BROTHER ROLAND (BR) | |
| --- | --- |
| PREV CLOSE | 35.78 |
| OPEN | 36.01 |
| BID | 33.57 x 100 |

#3
EXAMPLE

est.

Right now Brother Roland. (BR) is at $36.85 dollars a share; and as long as there is not a new low we know that it will go to $38.75: we just don't know when. The next thing I look at is the 52 week range and here on our example it says,

$31.36 (L) + $48.43 (H) = $79.79 / 2 = $39.89 Not a true 50%

What you're looking for is the 52 week low and comparing it to where the market is. The closer the stock gets to the 52 week low the better it is to buy or get in. Most of the time the stock goes past the 50% line before it stops climbing up. I use the 50% line as a place to get out.

You are the only person that needs to feel comfortable with your trade. For me the more space I have between where the 50% place is and where I buy is; the better my money can make money for me. If there is less than a $5.00 dollar move between the 50% mark and where the market is then look for a better trade. That's why we have more than one stock to trade with.

Say you go in and the 50% mark is only $3.00 dollars away from where you bought or got in. What happens if your stock goes down $2.00 dollars before it starts to go up? The 50% mark would have changed making your money making margin even smaller. Almost every time I buy a stock it almost always goes down .50 cents to $1.00 dollar within 20 minutes.

Just because a stock price gets close to a new low it doesn't mean it is ready to go up. What can you do? Say you have $10, 000.00 dollars to trade with and the stock is at a new low at $10.00 dollars a share; you can go in and spend $1,000.00 dollars buying that stock. Let's say it goes down to $9.00 dollars a share, than you spend $2,000.00 more Then it goes back up to $10.00 a share, now might be a good time to go all in. The more familiar you know a stock the easier it will be the next time you trade it.

All this takes time for you to get the confidantes you need to go all in or not.

If you make small buys at first, it will allow you to have more money to buy with when the stock bottoms out. I like to buy 1000 stocks at a time, because every time the stock goes up $1.00 dollar, I make $1000.00 dollars. The more you work at reading your charts and follow all the criteria's in this book: your money will make money for you every time.

Some money is better than no money. Don't get greedy and don't sell your trade just because that stock took a $2.00 or $3.00 dollar mud dive. If you followed and did your homework and the 50% mark does not go below the place you bought the stock at, than just wait it will hit the 50% mark if you let it.

I play it safe and almost always get out after the stock makes $1.00 or $2.00 dollars. (Some money is always better than no money.) This one criteria alone may be your biggest criteria of all. . .

# CHAPTER SEVEN

# Where to go and get all the stocks you need

T he first thing I did was to go on line and looked up Dividends. The internet took me to a page with listings from what are the top ten dividends to all the stocks with dividends.

I went where I could find all the stocks with dividends between $10.00 dollars up to $30.00 dollars and the range was between 9.5% to 1%. Obviously because of the small amount of money we have when we first get started with; we don't need to be buying $100.00 dollar stocks. By doing this, it automatically gets all of our stocks to fit one of the four criteria's.

The next thing would be is to eliminate any of the stocks that did not fit all four criteria's. So I took all the stocks that made a 50 cent or more move on the 36 day history chart; and only the ones that made 20 or more hits out of 36 days and have been around for more than 10 years, I kept and put the rest in a different colored folder.

Once you have a larger retirement account, you may want to go back and find stock that range from $40.00 dollars to $100.00 dollars to play with, because they have larger dollar moves and they may be more stable. I have found out that most people that start buying and selling stocks by using this book; once they start making money they start buying five or more stocks at the same time.

This is fine if you want to pay more commissions to your brokerage firm and have less money to make money for you. I am just as guilty as they are; in my first year of buying and selling stocks, I must have paid over $1,000.00 dollars in commissions. In my second year of buying and selling stocks I spent less than $50.00 dollars in commissions and I made close to the same amount of money. If you do the math, you will see that you have a lot more money to make money with by making one buy and sell at a time.

Because most of your stocks are fast movers, (they go up and down) 20 or more times out of 36 days: you will be buying and selling sometimes on the same day. Don't take this the wrong way, you can sell a stock and buy a different one on the same day, but you will have to wait three to four days before you can sell the new stock you just bought. There is no getting around the three to five business days for your money to be accounted for as clean and clear funds. and if your stock goes down while you are waiting? This may not be the way you make your next trade. If you look at the next page, you will see two charts. If you look at chart # 2, you can see how the stock can only go three ways, up, down and sideways You can also see how many times this stock moved up more than 5.00 dollar to make money for you.

Now if you look at chart #1, you will see that all the graphs will show you similar patterns. It's all most like watching an ocean waves going up and down. The more graphs that you look at the easier it will get for you to read. If you look at chart #2 you can see that it's not time to buy: but if you look at chart #1 and each one of those bumps are 5.00 dollar moves or more you might want to buy this stock.

By the way, if you look at chart # 1 and chart # 2 a little closer, you will see that most of the time when one is going up the other one is going down. When you're not trading in # 1, you might be trading in # 2. If you are still not shore, there are two other indicators you can go to.

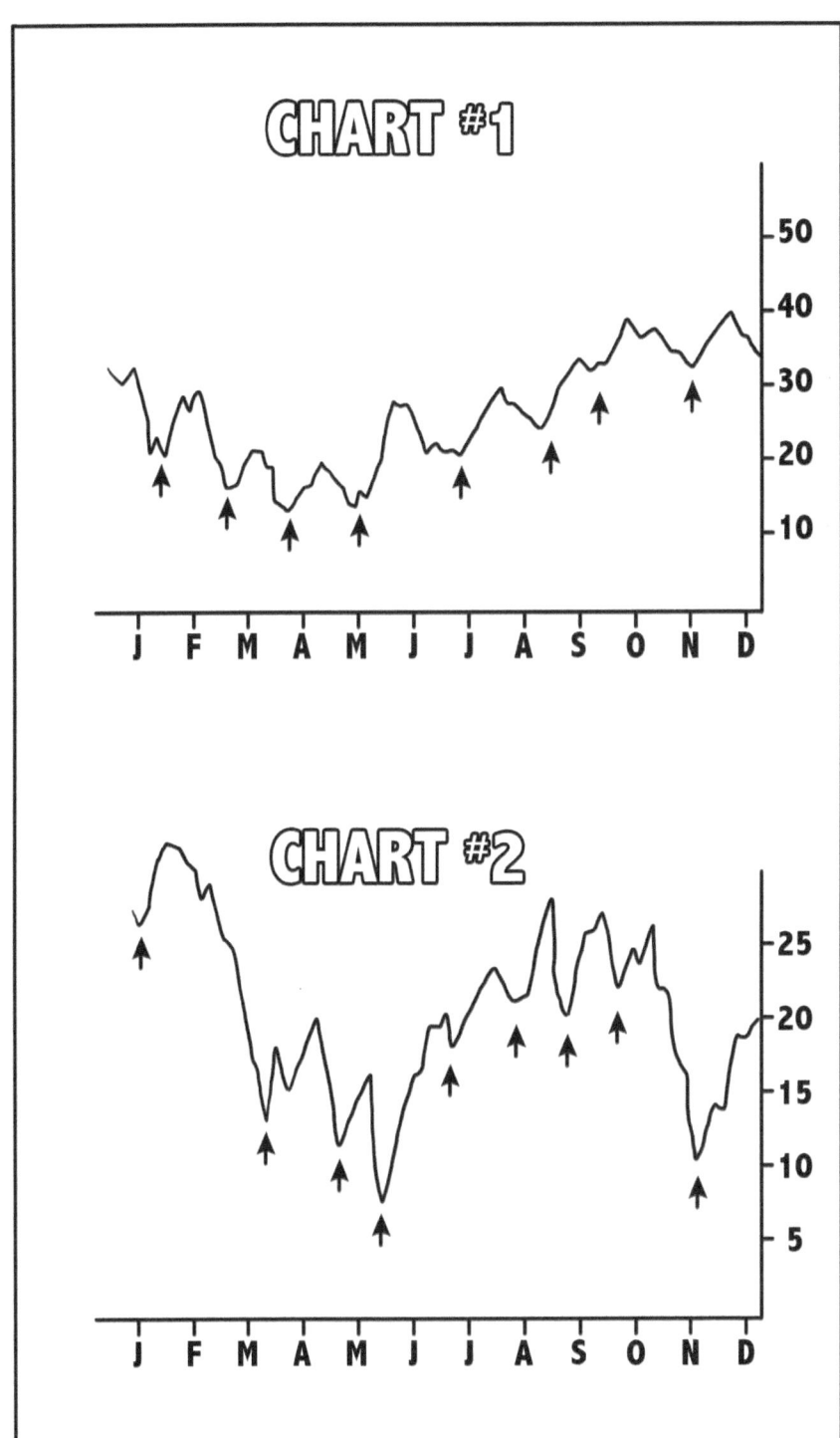

Let's have a closer look at this, shall we?

If you look at chart # 1, you can see that both the Dow and the Nasdaq are showing us that they are down. If we look at chart #2, it clearly shows us that the Dow, Nasdaq and S&P have all taken a large mud dive. This would indicate that it's not a good time to buy. You may want to wait until the market indicators are in the + before buying.

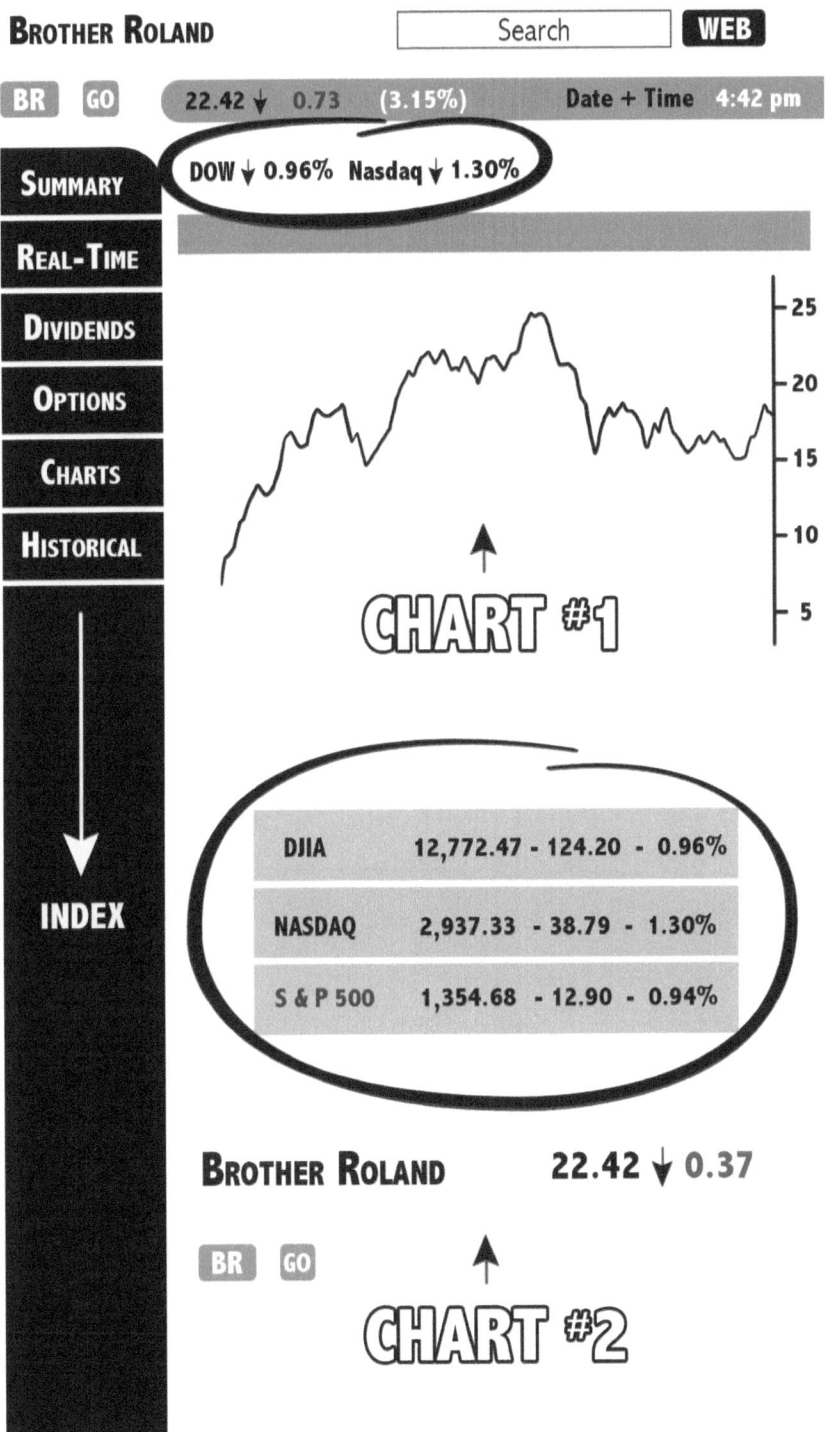

BROTHER ROLAND

Search          WEB

BR   GO          22.42 ↓ 0.73   (3.15%)        Date + Time   4:42 pm

DOW ↓ 0.96%   Nasdaq ↓ 1.30%

SUMMARY

REAL-TIME

DIVIDENDS

OPTIONS

CHARTS

HISTORICAL

25
20
15
10
5

↑
CHART #1

↓
INDEX

| DJIA | 12,772.47 - 124.20 - 0.96% |
| NASDAQ | 2,937.33 - 38.79 - 1.30% |
| S & P 500 | 1,354.68 - 12.90 - 0.94% |

BROTHER ROLAND          22.42 ↓ 0.37

BR   GO          ↑
CHART #2

Until you become familiar with the stock you want, your best bet is to go on line using a computer with a printer to find all the stocks you want to make money for you that meet all of the criteria's.

The charts tell you everything you need to know by just looking at them. In time, they will be talking to you. At this time I would have seven different stocks printed out for you to start your portfolio with and then I would ask you to go on line and find me three more stocks that follows all of these criteria that I showed you. Then I would have you find the true 50% line and I would like you to tell me when you would buy these stocks and when you would sell them.

Because I am not there with you and cannot use any brand names or even print out any pictures for you, I will show you how I play a stock that goes up, down and sideways. Take a look at chart # 1 on the next page. This is a stock that goes up. Everyone wishes they can find a stock like this one; because all they have to do is buy it and watch their money grow.

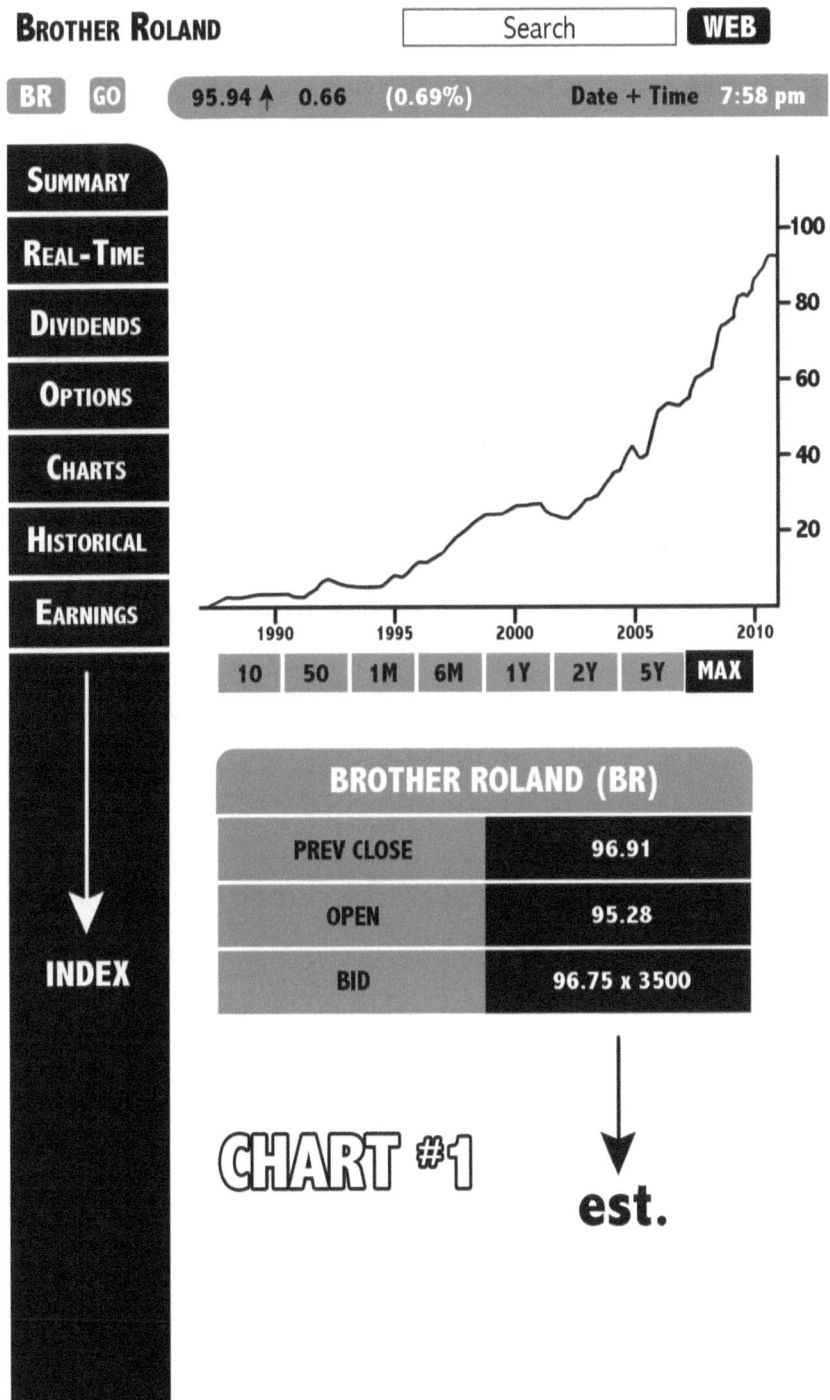

**BROTHER ROLAND**

Search | WEB

BR | GO | 95.94 ↑ 0.66 (0.69%) | Date + Time 7:58 pm

SUMMARY
REAL-TIME
DIVIDENDS
OPTIONS
CHARTS
HISTORICAL
EARNINGS

↓

INDEX

| | | | | | | | |
| 10 | 50 | 1M | 6M | 1Y | 2Y | 5Y | MAX |

| BROTHER ROLAND (BR) | |
| --- | --- |
| PREV CLOSE | 96.91 |
| OPEN | 95.28 |
| BID | 96.75 x 3500 |

CHART #1

↓

est.

Let's look at chart # 2, shall we?

As you can see, as long as the stock is going up you're all in, but what do you do if the stock takes a mud dive? If the stock goes down more than ten % from the new high; you may want to get out. Every four or five years the stock market turns from + to -. Some stocks may go down more than others.

The good news is that if the stock goes down a lot and makes a large 50% mark and you know where the stock will go then all you have to do is wait until the stock goes up and get in. This is how you would trade a stock that goes down.

BROTHER ROLAND

Search  **WEB**

BR  GO

Date + Time

SUMMARY

REAL-TIME

DIVIDENDS

OPTIONS

CHARTS

HISTORICAL

EARNINGS

INDEX

GET
OUT

GOT
IN

50% →

100
80
60
40
20

1980  1985  1990  1995  2000  2005  2010

| 10 | 50 | 1M | 6M | 1Y | 2Y | 5Y | MAX |

| BROTHER ROLAND (BR) | |
|---|---|
| PREV CLOSE | 41.50 |
| OPEN | 40.28 |
| BID | 41.32 x 100 |

CHART #2

est.

Now! Let's have a look at chart # 3, shall we?

As you can see the stock is going sideways. This is my favorite kind of stock to trade. If you look at chart # 4 we already know that the 50% mark is at $ 17.00 dollars and the graph shows us that it has not hit that mark for over 6 months.

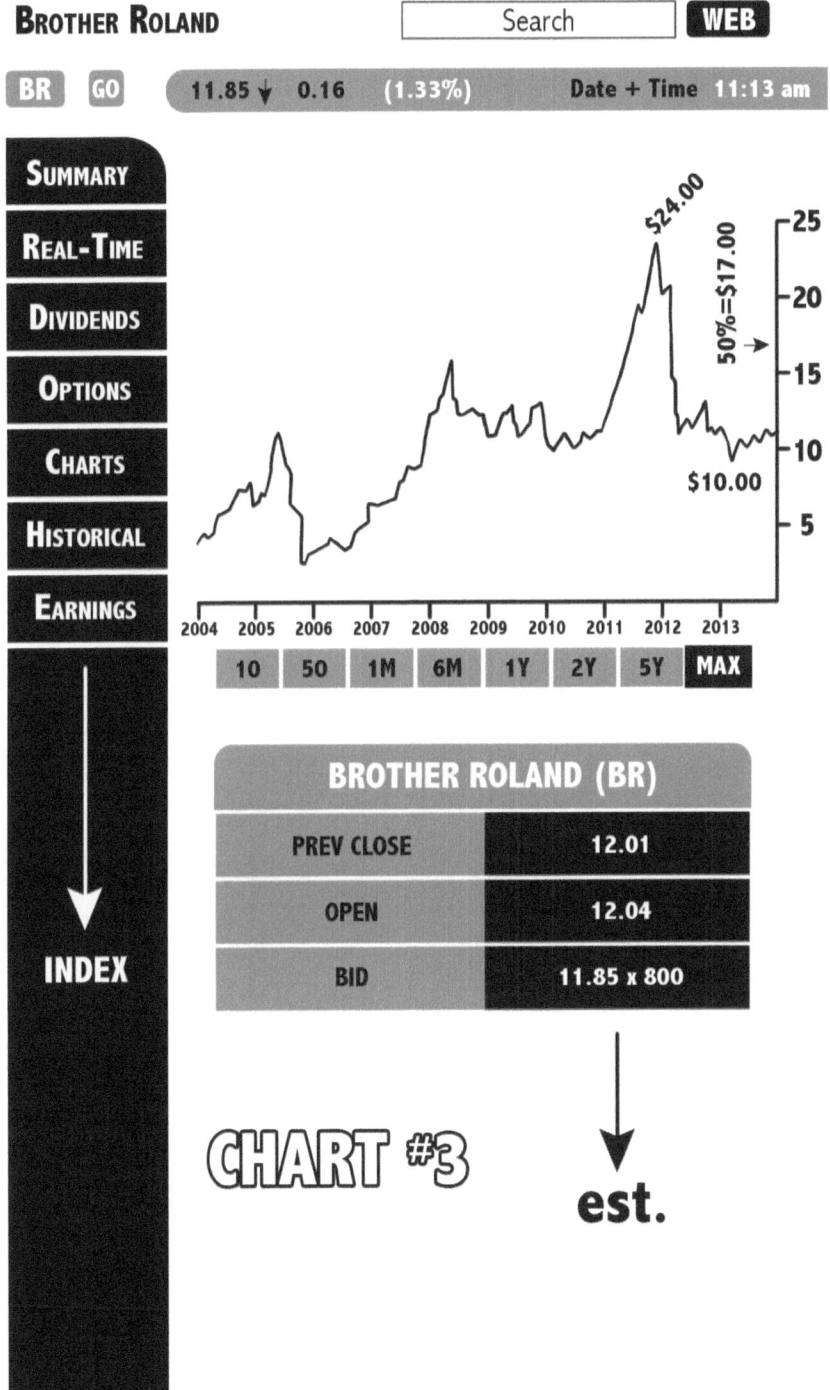

Now look at chart # 5. You will see a window where you can get in and out by buying and selling this stock. Let's say you buy 1,000 shares at $12.50 dollars a share and you sell them at $13.50 dollars a share. How much money did your money make for you?

$$1,000 \times \$1.00 = \$1,000.00 \text{ dollars.}$$

What would happen if you buy 10,000 shares?

$$10,000 \times \$1.00 = \$10,000.00 \text{ dollars.}$$

The cheaper the stock is, the more stocks you can buy. All you would need is three or four stocks like this one and you will never have to go anywhere else. I had played a stock like this one; and after six trades, I had more than doubled my money.

You can't learn how to do the treading unless you do it yourself; no one is going to do it for you. In order to have your money making money for you; you're going to need faith in all of the instructions given to you in this book.

God bless you two folds

*Brother Roland*

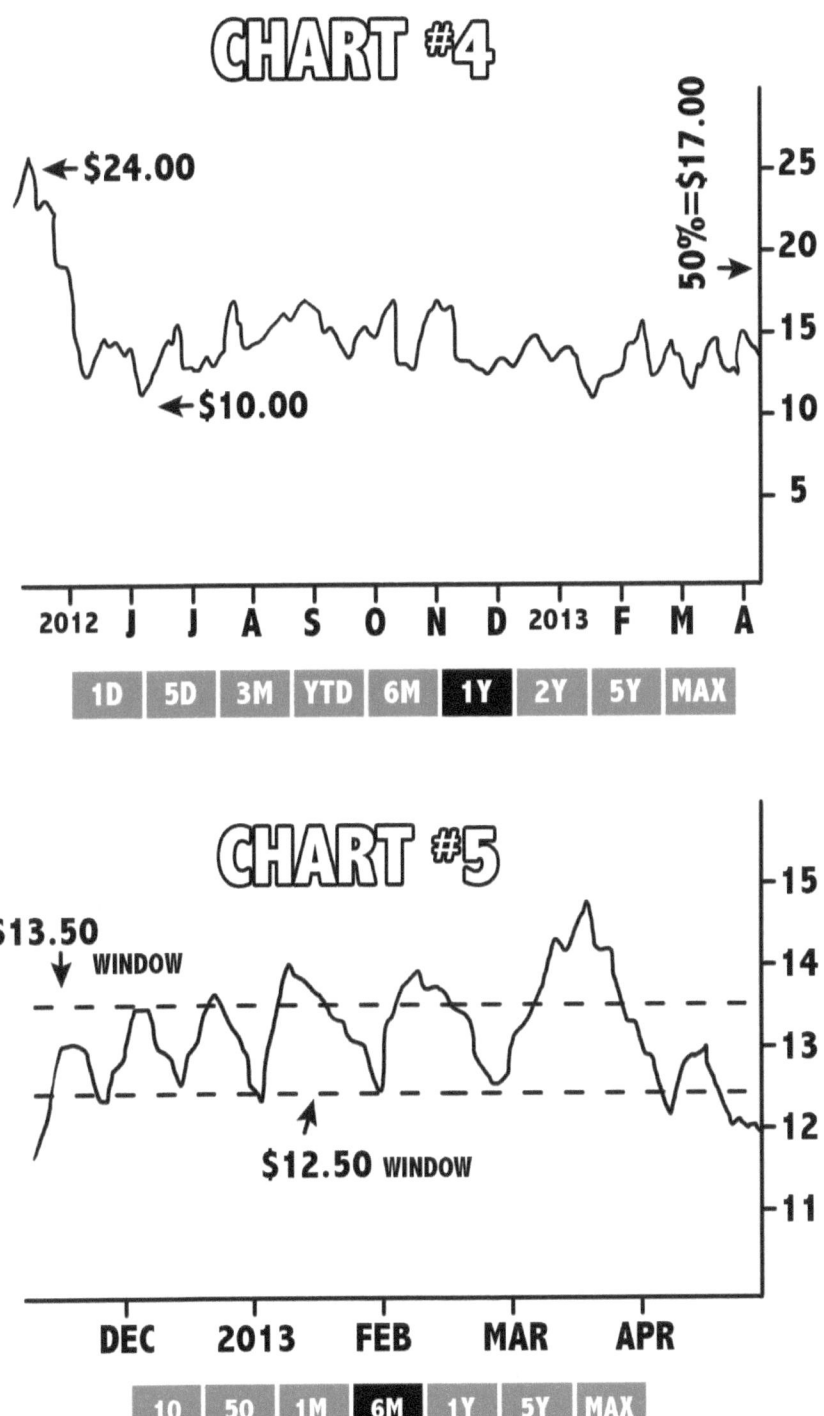

# About The Author

You might say, I grew up in a God fearing home along with my three other brothers and three sisters. Our Dad took us to church every weak except when he had to work; and we had to walk to a closer church down the street because he had the car. Around the age of ten or eleven I went to church and one of the elders told me that I was not allowed to go to his church anymore; because I belonged to the other church down the street. As a child, I couldn't understand why his church took my money all those years and then they kicked me out of God's house?

Some five or six years later when I started working full time and still going to school; going to a church that didn't want me anymore was not big on my priority list of things to do. Some twenty five or so years later one of my sisters wanted to talk to me about God's word. Although I knew that the Lord was always with me: I told her, That I was doing just fine without Him; and when I get older I would go to church every day like Dad if that's what the Lord wanted. Not knowing what I had just done, it wasn't but a day or two later that my whole life was turned upside down.

You see, everything that I thought was important and had put before the Lord was taken from me. My houses, my new cars, my good paying job. Does this sound like anyone you know? I was one of those people who needed a two by ten, instead of a two by four to get rid of the stinking thinking. Finely I gave my life to the Lord and started going to church every time the doors were open and read my bible every day.

Just when I thought everything was the way the Lord wanted my life to be: my wife told me, She wanted to be put first and that I had to choose between her or the Lord. You can almost feel the love, can't you? Because I continued to put God first in my life and my wife second, she left me for someone else; and because I put my two children third, they left me as well; but because I put God first, He showed me how to buy and sell stocks. I now own and live in a brand new house with new furniture and I have a new car free and clear. No debts and I was able to retire at the age of fifty five. Now all my time is His time.

That's enough about me: now it's all about you. If you have read this whole book up to this point; then know this, whatsoever the Lord did for me, He can do for you and even more. Just don't wait until a two by ten is needed to get rid of your stinking thinking. Amen . . .

I love you in the Lord always

*Brother Roland*

www.ingramcontent.com/pod-product-compliance
Lightning Source LLC
Chambersburg PA
CBHW030911180526
45163CB00004B/1788